One-Hour Amigurumi

Amigurumi

40 Cute & Quick Crochet Patterns with Minimal Sewing

Melanie Morita-Hu

author of *Hooked on Amigurumi* and founder of Knot Too Shabby Crochet

PAGE STREET
PUBLISHING CO.

PAGE STREET
PUBLISHING CO.

Copyright © 2022 Melanie Morita-Hu

First published in 2022 by
Page Street Publishing Co.
27 Congress Street, Suite 1511
Salem, MA 01970
www.pagestreetpublishing.com

Distributed by Macmillan, sales in Canada by The Canadian Manda Group.

26 25 24 23 22   1 2 3 4 5

ISBN-13: 978-1-64567-666-9
ISBN-10: 1-64567-666-8

Library of Congress Control Number: 2022935239

Cover and book design by Rosie Stewart for Page Street Publishing Co.
Photography by Melanie Morita-Hu

Printed and bound in the United States of America

To the future little family that we hope to build one day, whenever and however you finally decide to join us: I hope this book serves as a small reminder of just how much you are loved and inspires you to pursue your dreams and cherish every moment along the way.

Table of Contents

Introduction

Every amigurumi maker will eventually come to a point where they are left with a pile of half-finished projects and stray limbs, either because they're tired of spending night after night on the same design, or because of the tedious monotony of SEWING! After making my first few pieces, I quickly came to realize this wasn't the way I wanted to design and create amigurumi. Thus began my endeavor to find an easier, faster solution!

One-Hour Amigurumi is all about using unique shortcuts, techniques and skills to minimize sewing, reduce construction time and create beautiful seamless pieces in just one hour or less. You can whip up one of these adorable designs between chores, while binge-watching your favorite show or during a long road trip.

This is my preferred approach to amigurumi, and it's what inspired my small business, Knot Too Shabby Crochet. Since then, I've been designing and selling patterns through my Etsy shop and sharing fun creations on my Instagram account, @knottooshabbycrochet. This eventually led to me writing my first book, *Hooked on Amigurumi*, which has been flying off the shelves at major retailers, including Joann, Michaels, Amazon and more. With the success of my first book, it was clear that the world loves simple, no-sew patterns, and a second book seemed like a no-brainer!

In this book, I will take you step by step through 40 of my favorite quick and easy patterns. While these projects are designed to be completed in an hour by your average experienced crocheter, everyone works at their own pace. Those who enjoy a slower crochet pace or those who are less experienced might want to set aside a little extra time.

As you flip through the book, you'll notice that it's organized into chapters, each based on my life experiences, hobbies and passions: "Aloha State of Mind," "A Little Dirt Never Hurt," "What's Cookin', Good Lookin'?" and "Celebrate the Season." Each chapter includes a variety of adorable patterns around a particular theme. Many of the designs also pair perfectly with the no-sew designs from my previous book, *Hooked on Amigurumi*!

Each chapter includes patterns of varying levels of difficulty, starting from level 1 (easiest) to level 3 (hardest). If you are new to amigurumi, I recommend starting with some of the level 1 patterns. Level 2 and level 3 patterns typically use special no-sew techniques that will be indicated in my introduction to each pattern, so beginners may want to take some time to review that information before getting started. You can reference the project-by-skill-level section in the back of the book (page 146) to develop a game plan that best meets your level of experience. If you are looking to learn the basics or need a refresher, check out the back of the book (page 137) for a crash course in all things amigurumi. In that section, I also share my favorite supplies and cover some of the basics to get you started.

The patterns in this book are bright, colorful, fun and designed specifically to keep sewing to a minimum. These cute and simple patterns are also perfect for scaling up to any size. Instead of Paintbox Cotton Aran Yarn, try using Hobbii Baby Snuggle Solid Yarn and a larger hook to make big, squishy, cuddle-sized versions of your favorites! I love seeing all your finished pieces, so don't forget to tag me on Instagram at @knottooshabbycrochet.

Happy crocheting, friends! *Melanie Morita Hu*

Aloha
State of Mind

As you may know from my first book, my parents grew up in Hawaii! They now live on the mainland, but we try to go back to Oahu and visit our families whenever we can. The visits are always filled with tons of food and time with family. The aunties, uncles and cousins all get together on my auntie's deck with the most gorgeous view overlooking the beach. Then, we feast on some Hawaiian and local classics, like lau lau, poke, poi, kalua pork, lomi lomi, mac salad, Spam® musubi and so much more. Or we visit my grandparents' house and explore their yard filled with tropical plants, koi fish, turtles, birds and so many other fun things to discover.

In between family time, we love to explore the island, go snorkeling, lie in the sun, hike and just take in all the beauty the island has to offer. This chapter encapsulates all those carefree summer moments, so relax and unwind with these fun and easy projects. Although these patterns were designed to be completed in an hour, we're on Aloha time here, so feel free to take it slow and enjoy! From Breezy the Palm Tree (page 29) to Kona the Shave Ice (page 17) and Stella the Sun (page 11), I give you all the beachy vibes to get you in that Aloha state of mind.

Skill Level: 2

Materials

0.5 oz Paintbox Yarns Cotton Aran in Blood Orange (or similar worsted weight/aran yarn)

0.5 oz Paintbox Yarns Cotton Aran in Buttercup Yellow (or similar worsted weight/aran yarn)

Size E-4 (3.5-mm) crochet hook

Stitch marker for marking the first st

2 (¼" [6-mm]) black plastic safety eyes

Scrap piece of black yarn for embroidery

Polyester fiberfill

Tapestry needle

Terminology

R1: row 1 or round 1

st(s): stitch(es)

ch: chain

sc: single crochet

inc: single crochet increase

dec: invisible decrease

MR: magic ring

Stella the Sun

On warm summer days, my pups love to take long naps in the sun. They are crazy maniacs 83 percent of the time, but when they're sunbathing and their sleepy little eyes can hardly stay open, they are my little rays of sunshine. Stella the Sun is uniquely designed to cut down on time and work up quickly while you relax and lounge under the warm sun. The sun rays are made first, then they are worked into the center of the sun with no sewing necessary. Check out the Stitches and Techniques section (page 139) for tips on how to single crochet through multiple pieces. Stella's finished size is approximately 4 inches (10 cm) in diameter and 1½ inches (4 cm) thick.

Sun Ray (x9)

This piece starts at the tip of each sunray, using Blood Orange yarn.

R1: 4 sc in MR (4)

R2: [1 sc, 1 inc] x2 (6)

R3: [2 sc, 1 inc] x2 (8)

R4: Ch 1, flatten the piece, then working through the front and backstitches together, 4 sc (4)

Ch 1 and fasten off. There is no need to weave in the ends; the yarn will end up inside the piece.

(continued)

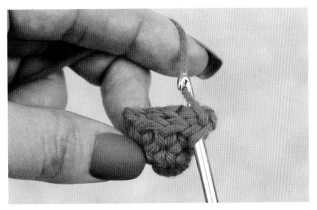

Sun ray, round 4

Sun

This piece starts at the center of the sun, using Buttercup Yellow yarn.

R1: 6 sc in MR (6)

R2: 1 inc in each st (12)

R3: [1 sc, 1 inc] x6 (18)

R4: [2 sc, 1 inc] x6 (24)

R5: [3 sc, 1 inc] x6 (30)

R6: [4 sc, 1 inc] x6 (36)

R7: 1 sc in each st (36)

R8: [working through each sun ray and the sun together, sc 4] x9 (36)

R9: 1 sc in each st (36)

Place the eyes between R3 and R4, about 4 stitches apart. Using black yarn, embroider the mouth onto the front of the face, just below the eyes, using the tapestry needle.

R10: [4 sc, 1 dec] x6 (30)

R11: [3 sc, 1 dec] x6 (24)

R12: [2 sc, 1 dec] x6 (18)

R13: [1 sc, 1 dec] x6 (12)

Stuff the piece with polyester fiberfill.

R14: 6 dec (6)

Close off, and then hide the yarn end with a tapestry needle.

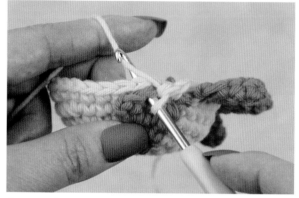

Sun, round 8

Stella the Sun, finished

Skill Level: 3

Materials

0.5 oz Paintbox Yarns Cotton Aran in Pistachio (or similar worsted weight/ aran yarn)

1 oz Paintbox Yarns Cotton Aran in Daffodil Yellow (or similar worsted weight/ aran yarn)

Size E-4 (3.5-mm) crochet hook

Stitch marker for marking the first st

2 (¼" [6-mm]) black plastic safety eyes

Scrap piece of black yarn for embroidery

Polyester fiberfill

Tapestry needle

Terminology

R1: row 1 or round 1

st(s): stitch(es)

ch: chain

slst: slip stitch

sc: single crochet

hdc: half double crochet

inc: single crochet increase

dec: invisible decrease

MR: magic ring

Sunny the Pineapple

Even though my parents grew up in Hawaii, they'd always pick at least one tourist attraction to visit every time we made a trip back. I remember running through the Dole Plantation Pineapple Garden Maze for hours, then ending the day with some fresh pineapple or a frosty Dole Whip. This adorable pineapple pattern perfectly encapsulates those carefree days in the sun. Sunny was designed to be a quick and seamless piece with no sewing necessary. The leaves are made first as one continuous piece and worked into the main body of the pineapple. Then, the body is worked as a series of bobble stitches to create the pineapple texture. If you're not familiar with the bobble stitch, this pattern may take a little longer, but I have provided instructions and photos to help you through it! Sunny's finished size is approximately 4½ inches (11.5 cm) tall and 2½ inches (6.5 cm) wide.

Pineapple Leaves

This piece starts at one end of the leaves, using Pistachio yarn.

Ch 19,

R1: Starting at the second chain from the hook, 18 sc (18)

R2: Ch 1, turn, [ch 9, starting at the second chain from the hook, 1 slst, 1 sc, 6 hdc, skip 1 sc of the foundation stitches, 1 slst in next foundation stitch] x9 to create a total of 9 leaves

Ch 1 and fasten off. There is no need to weave in the ends; the yarn will end up inside the piece.

(continued)

Leaves, finished

Pineapple

This piece starts at the top of the pineapple, using Daffodil Yellow yarn.

R1: 6 sc in MR (6)

Hold the leaves and pineapple together as shown so that the leaves curl outward.

R2: Working through the foundation chain of the leaves and pineapple together, 1 inc in each st (12)

R3: Working through the foundation chain of the leaves and pineapple together, [1 sc, 1 inc] x6 (18)

R4: [5 sc, 1 inc] x3 (21)

For this pattern, we will also be using a bobble stitch to create the texture of the pineapple. To create a bobble stitch, yarn over, insert the hook into the stitch, yarn over, pull up a loop, yarn over, pull through the first 2 loops, then (yarn over, insert hook in the same stitch or space, yarn over, pull up a loop, yarn over, pull through the first 2 loops) 2 more times. There will be 4 loops on the hook. Yarn over and draw the yarn through all the loops on the hook.

R5: 1 bobble stitch, then [1 sc, 1 bobble stitch] x10 (21)

R6: 1 sc, then [1 bobble stitch, 1 sc] x10 (21)

R7: 1 bobble stitch, then [1 sc, 1 bobble stitch] x10 (21)

R8: 1 sc, then [1 bobble stitch, 1 sc] x10 (21)

R9: 1 bobble stitch, then [1 sc, 1 bobble stitch] x10 (21)

R10: 1 sc, then [1 bobble stitch, 1 sc] x10 (21)

R11: 1 bobble stitch, then [1 sc, 1 bobble stitch] x10 (21)

Place the eyes between R7 and R8, about 4 stitches apart. Using black yarn, embroider the mouth onto the front of the face, just below the eyes, using the tapestry needle. Stuff the piece with polyester fiberfill.

R12: [5 sc, 1 dec] x3 (18)

R13: [1 sc, 1 dec] x6 (12)

R14: 6 dec (6)

Close off, and then hide the yarn end with a tapestry needle.

Pineapple, rounds 2 and 3

Pineapple, bobble stitch

Materials

0.5 oz Paintbox Yarns Cotton Aran in Paper White (or similar worsted weight/aran yarn)

0.5 oz Paintbox Yarns Cotton Aran in Pillar Red (or similar worsted weight/aran yarn)

0.5 oz Paintbox Yarns Cotton Aran in Buttercup Yellow (or similar worsted weight/aran yarn)

0.5 oz Paintbox Yarns Cotton Aran in Kingfisher Blue (or similar worsted weight/aran yarn)

Size E-4 (3.5-mm) crochet hook

Stitch marker for marking the first st

2 (¼" [6-mm]) black plastic safety eyes

Scrap piece of black yarn for embroidery

Polyester fiberfill

Tapestry needle

Kona the Shave Ice

On every trip back to the islands, my family and I would make it a point to drive to the north shore for some of the best shave ice in town. The mountain of powdery soft shave ice with sticky sweet syrup and a big scoop of vanilla ice cream at the bottom was absolute perfection, just like Kona the Shave Ice. For this pattern, we start with the base of the cone, leaving a row of free loops to attach the shave ice, then a series of color changes to create each flavor. These techniques might be a bit tricky at first, but I'll walk you through them! This pattern calls for red, yellow and blue yarn, but feel free to personalize your cone! Kona's finished size is approximately 3½ inches (9 cm) tall and 2½ inches (6.5 cm) wide.

Terminology

R1: row 1 or round 1

st(s): stitch(es)

slst: slip stitch

sc: single crochet

inc: single crochet increase

dec: invisible decrease

MR: magic ring

FLO: front loops only

Cone

This piece starts at the bottom of the cone using Paper White yarn.

R1: 6 sc in MR (6)

R2: [1 sc, 1 inc] x3 (9)

R3: [2 sc, 1 inc] x3 (12)

R4: [3 sc, 1 inc] x3 (15)

R5: [4 sc, 1 inc] x3 (18)

R6: [5 sc, 1 inc] x3 (21)

R7: [6 sc, 1 inc] x3 (24)

R8: [7 sc, 1 inc] x3 (27)

(continued)

R9: [8 sc, 1 inc] x3 (30)

R10: Working in FLO, [9 sc, 1 inc] x3 (33)

Slst in next st. Fasten off and weave in the ends with a tapestry needle.

Place the eyes between R6 and R7, about 4 stitches apart. Using black yarn, embroider the mouth onto the front of the face with a tapestry needle, just below the eyes.

Shave Ice

Using Pillar Red Yarn, join the yarn to the first back loop of R9 left behind from R10 of the cone, ch 1, then start your first stitch in the same stitch as the join.

For the following rounds, change the yarn from Pillar Red to Buttercup Yellow to Kingfisher Blue at each repeat. Then, start the next round with Pillar Red again and repeat the color changes in the same order. Refer to page 143 for more information on color changes. There is no need to cut the old color and tie the ends together inside the piece; just drop the yarn inside the piece when it is not being used, and pick up the yarn again for the next color change.

R1: Working into the BLO from R9, [4 sc, 1 inc, 4 sc, 1 inc] x3, changing colors each repeat (36)

R2–6: [12 sc] x3, changing colors each repeat (36)

R7: [4 sc, 1 dec, 4 sc, 1 dec] x3, changing colors each repeat (30)

R8: [3 sc, 1 dec, 3 sc, 1 dec] x3, changing colors each repeat (24)

R9: [2 sc, 1 dec, 2 sc, 1 dec] x3, changing colors each repeat (18)

R10: [1 sc, 1 dec, 1 sc, 1 dec] x3, changing colors each repeat (12)

Stuff the piece with polyester fiberfill.

R11: [2 dec] x3, changing colors each repeat (6)

Close off, and then hide the yarn end with a tapestry needle.

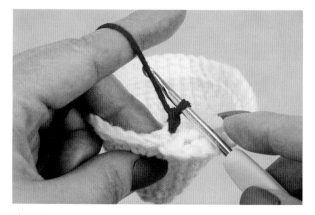

Shave ice, joining yarn

Kona the Shave Ice, finished

IZ the Rainbow

This pattern is named after the Hawaiian musical legend Israel "IZ" Kamakawiwoʻole and his captivating rendition of "Somewhere over the Rainbow/What a Wonderful World." My parents grew up in Hawaii and we'd listen to his album on repeat during car rides to school. So, when I got married, it only seemed fitting to use this song for my father-daughter dance. IZ's beautiful voice and gentle strumming have touched the hearts of so many people all over the world, including my own, and this pattern is an homage to him. IZ the Rainbow is worked as an oval, then folded in half and joined together to create its colorful arches. IZ's finished size is approximately 3 inches (7.5 cm) tall and 4½ inches (11.5 cm) wide.

Terminology

R1: row 1 or round 1

st(s): stitch(es)

ch: chain

slst: slip stitch

sc: single crochet

inc: single crochet increase

Rainbow

This piece starts at the middle of the rainbow, using Pale Lilac yarn to create an oval.

Ch 13,

R1: Starting at the second chain from the hook, 11 sc and 1 inc in the back loops, rotate the chain, then 11 sc and 1 inc in the front loops (26)

Switch to Kingfisher Blue yarn.

R2: 1 inc, 10 sc, 3 inc, 10 sc, 2 inc (32)

R3: [1 sc, 1 inc, 11 sc, 1 inc, 1 sc, 1 inc] x2 (38)

Switch to Grass Green yarn.

(continued)

R4: 1 sc, 1 inc, 12 sc, 1 inc, 2 sc, 1 inc, 2 sc, 1 inc, 12 sc, 1 inc, 2 sc, 1 inc, 1 sc (44)

R5: 2 sc, 1 inc, 13 sc, 1 inc, 3 sc, 1 inc, 3 sc, 1 inc, 13 sc, 1 inc, 3 sc, 1 inc, 1 sc (50)

Switch to Buttercup Yellow yarn.

R6: 3 sc, 1 inc, 14 sc, 1 inc, 4 sc, 1 inc, 4 sc, 1 inc, 14 sc, 1 inc, 4 sc, 1 inc, 1 sc (56)

R7: 4 sc, 1 inc, 15 sc, 1 inc, 5 sc, 1 inc, 5 sc, 1 inc, 15 sc, 1 inc, 5 sc, 1 inc, 1 sc (62)

Switch to Blood Orange yarn.

R8: 4 sc, 1 inc, 16 sc, 1 inc, 6 sc, 1 inc, 6 sc, 1 inc, 16 sc, 1 inc, 6 sc, 1 inc, 2 sc (68)

R9: 5 sc, 1 inc, 17 sc, 1 inc, 7 sc, 1 inc, 7 sc, 1 inc, 17 sc, 1 inc, 7 sc, 1 inc, 2 sc (74)

Switch to Pillar Red yarn.

R10: 6 sc, 1 inc, 18 sc, 1 inc, 8 sc, 1 inc, 8 sc, 1 inc, 18 sc, 1 inc, 8 sc, 1 inc, 2 sc (80)

Place the eyes between R2 and R3, as shown. Using black yarn, embroider the mouth onto the front of the face with a tapestry needle, just below the eyes.

After R10, work about 16 sc so you're lined up with the side of the rainbow. For the next row, lightly stuff the piece with polyester fiberfill as you go.

R11: Ch 1, fold the piece in half, then working through front and backstitches together, 9 sc, 1 inc, 9 sc, 1 inc, 9 sc, 1 inc, 10 sc (43)

Ch 1 to fasten off and weave in the ends with a tapestry needle.

Rainbow, round 11

IZ the Rainbow, finished

Skipper the Pool Float

The summer before college, I practically lived at the beach with my friends. One day, my friend was out in the water, jumping around and having a blast. But to the lifeguard on shore, it must have looked like she was struggling. So, he ran into the water with his life preserver to save my very confused friend. Skipper the Pool Float won't save you in an emergency, but you'll be able to whip him up almost as quickly as that lifeguard came to the rescue! Skipper starts with a chain and is worked in continuous rounds, alternating between red and white yarn, then joined together to create a donut shape. Because we use some unique techniques here, this pattern is one of the more challenging projects in the book. Skipper's finished size is approximately 3½ inches (9 cm) in diameter and 1½ inches (4 cm) thick.

Pool Float

This piece starts at the outside edge of the Pool Float using Paper White yarn. The next few rounds will require color changes between Paper White and Pillar Red as indicated below. Refer to page 143 for more information on color changes. There is no need to cut the old color and tie the ends together inside the piece; just drop the yarn inside the piece when it is not being used, and pick up the yarn again for the next color change.

Using Paper White yarn, Ch 48, then start R1 in the first chain, creating a loop.

R1: [Using white yarn, 4 sc, then using red yarn, 4 sc] x6 (48)

(continued)

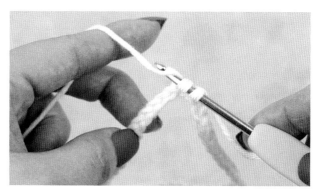

Pool float, round 1

R2: [Using white yarn, 4 sc, then using red yarn, 2 sc, 1 dec] x6 (42)

R3: [Using white yarn, 1 dec, 2 sc, then using red yarn, 3 sc] x6 (36)

R4: [Using white yarn, 3 sc, then using red yarn, 1 sc, 1 dec] x6 (30)

R5: [Using white yarn, 1 dec, 1 sc, then using red yarn, 2 sc] x6 (24)

R6-8: [Using white yarn, 2 sc, then using red yarn, 2 sc] x6 (24)

R9: [Using white yarn, 1 inc, 1 sc, then using red yarn, 2 sc] x6 (30)

R10: [Using white yarn, 3 sc, then using red yarn, 1 sc, 1 inc] x6 (36)

R11: [Using white yarn, 1 inc, 2 sc, then using red yarn, 3 sc] x6 (42)

R12: [Using white yarn, 4 sc, then using red yarn, 2 sc, 1 inc] x6 (48)

R13: [Using white yarn, 4 sc, then using red yarn, 4 sc] x6 (48)

Place the eyes between R3 and R4, about 4 stitches apart. Using black yarn, embroider the mouth onto the front of the face, just below the eyes, using the tapestry needle.

Switch to Paper White yarn.

R14: Working through R13 and the foundation chain together and stuffing periodically with the polyester fiberfill, 1 sc in each st (48)

Slst in next st. Fasten off and weave in the ends with a tapestry needle.

Pool float, round 14

Skipper the Pool Float, finished

Materials

0.5 oz Paintbox Yarns Cotton Aran in Paper White (or similar worsted weight/aran yarn)

0.5 oz Paintbox Yarns Cotton Aran in Pillar Red (or similar worsted weight/aran yarn)

0.5 oz Paintbox Yarns Cotton Aran in Buttercup Yellow (or similar worsted weight/aran yarn)

0.5 oz Paintbox Yarns Cotton Aran in Kingfisher Blue (or similar worsted weight/aran yarn)

Size E-4 (3.5-mm) crochet hook

Stitch marker for marking the first st

2 (¼" [6-mm]) black plastic safety eyes

Scrap piece of black yarn for embroidery

Polyester fiberfill

Tapestry needle

Terminology

R1: row 1 or round 1

st(s): stitch(es)

sc: single crochet

inc: single crochet increase

dec: invisible decrease

MR: magic ring

Spike the Beach Ball

Summers at the pool were always a blast when I was growing up, and nothing screams pool party like a classic blue, yellow and red beach ball. Spike the Beach Ball is a fun and easy pattern that can be worked up in no time at all. The only tricky part is that it involves a lot of color changes. If you need a refresher on color changes, feel free to check out the Stitches and Techniques section (page 139). But once you get the hang of it, I'm sure you'll have a ball! Spike's finished size is approximately 2½ inches (6.5 cm) in diameter.

Beach Ball

This piece starts at the center of the beach ball, using Paper White yarn.

R1: 6 sc in MR (6)

R2: 1 inc in each st (12)

R3: [1 sc, 1 inc] x6 (18)

For the following rows, change the yarn from Paper White, Pillar Red, Paper White, Buttercup Yellow, Paper White, to Kingfisher Blue at each repeat. Then, start the next round with Paper White again and repeat the color changes in the same order. Refer to page 143 for more information on color changes. There is no need to cut the old color and tie the ends together inside the piece; just drop the yarn inside the piece when it is not being used, and pick up the yarn again for the next color change.

R4: [2 sc, 1 inc] x6, changing colors each repeat (24)

R5: [3 sc, 1 inc] x6, changing colors each repeat (30)

R6: [4 sc, 1 inc] x6, changing colors each repeat (36)

R7–10: [6 sc in each] x6, changing colors each repeat (36)

R11: [1 dec, 4 sc] x6, changing colors each repeat (30)

R12: [1 dec, 3 sc] x6, changing colors each repeat (24)

(continued)

Place the eyes between R8 and R9, about 4 stitches apart. Using black yarn, embroider the mouth onto the front of the face with a tapestry needle, just below the eyes. Stuff the piece with polyester fiberfill.

Continue with Paper White yarn.

R13: [2 sc, 1 dec] x6 (18)

R14: [1 sc, 1 dec] x6 (12)

R15: 6 dec (6)

Close off, and then hide the yarn end with a tapestry needle.

Beach ball, top

Spike the Beach Ball, finished

Breezy the Palm Tree

Whenever we visit the islands, my jungle man of a husband insists on climbing every palm tree to collect coconuts. Then, he'll husk them right on the beach and crack them open. They are delicious and refreshing, but I'm amazed he hasn't hurt himself yet! While this pattern doesn't include any coconuts, Breezy the Palm Tree can be a bit tricky on your first try, so set aside some extra time if you're newer to amigurumi. The leaves are made first, then worked into the tree trunk to create a quick, no-sew piece. Breezy's finished size is approximately 5 inches (12.5 cm) tall and 1½ inches (4 cm) wide.

Leaves

This piece starts at one end of the leaves, using Pistachio yarn.

Ch 19,

R1: Starting at the second chain from the hook, 18 sc (18)

R2: Ch 1, turn, [ch 9, starting at the second chain from the hook, 1 slst, 1 sc, 6 hdc, skip 1 sc of the foundation stitches, 1 slst in next foundation stitch] x9 to create a total of 9 leaves

Ch 1 and fasten off. There is no need to weave in the ends; the yarn will end up inside the piece.

(continued)

Leaves, finished

Trunk

This piece starts at the top of the trunk, using Soft Fudge yarn.

R1: 6 sc in MR (6)

Hold the leaves and trunk together as shown so that the leaves curl outward.

R2: Working through the foundation chain of the leaves and trunk together, 1 inc in each st (12)

R3: Working through the foundation chain of the leaves and trunk together, 1 sc in each st (12)

R4-12: 1 sc in each st (12)

R13: [3 sc, 1 inc] x3 (15)

R14: 1 sc in each st (15)

R15: [4 sc, 1 inc] x3 (18)

R16: 1 sc in each st (18)

Place the eyes between R13 and R14, about 4 stitches apart. Using black yarn, embroider the mouth onto the front of the face with a tapestry needle, just below the eyes. Stuff the piece with polyester fiberfill.

R17: Working in BLO, [1 sc, 1 sc2tog] x6 (12)

R18: 6 dec (6)

Close off, and then hide the yarn end with a tapestry needle.

Trunk, rounds 2 and 3

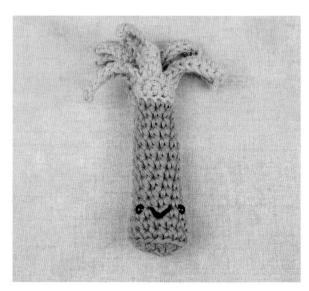

Breezy the Palm Tree, finished

Skill Level: 3

Materials

0.5 oz Paintbox Yarns Cotton Aran in Blood Orange (or similar worsted weight/aran yarn)

0.5 oz Paintbox Yarns Cotton Aran in Paper White (or similar worsted weight/aran yarn)

Size E-4 (3.5-mm) crochet hook

Stitch marker for marking the first st

2 (¼" [6-mm]) black plastic safety eyes

Polyester fiberfill

Tapestry needle

Terminology

R1: row 1 or round 1

st(s): stitch(es)

ch: chain

slst: slip stitch

sc: single crochet

inc: single crochet increase

dec: invisible decrease

MR: magic ring

Finn the Fish

Snorkeling is one of my favorite things to do when I visit the islands. We'll head out to the water almost every chance we get to explore the reef and chase colorful sea creatures, like Finn the Fish, as they dart through the ocean. Finn uses a few different techniques, so you may want to set aside some extra time for your first try. Working in the back loops of the chain to create the shape, attaching the fins and the series of repeating color changes may take some practice! This pattern starts at the tail and uses chain stitches to create the fins. Finn's finished size is approximately 4 inches (10 cm) long and 3 inches (7.5 cm) tall.

Fins (x2)

This piece starts at the center of each fin, using Blood Orange yarn. Repeat until you have two fins.

R1: 6 sc in MR (6)

Slst in next st and fasten off. There is no need to weave in the ends; the yarn will end up inside the piece.

(continued)

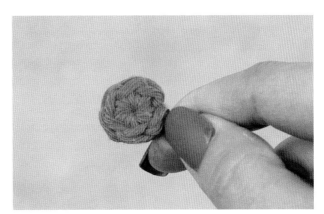

Fins, finished

Fish

This piece starts at the back of the fish, using Paper White yarn.

Ch 7,

R1: Starting in the second chain from the hook, 6 sc in back loops, rotate the chain, 6 sc in front loops (12)

R2: [2 sc, 1 dec] x3 (9)

Switch to Blood Orange yarn.

R3: 1 sc in each st (9)

R4: [1 sc, 1 dec] x3 (6)

Switch to Paper White yarn.

R5: 1 sc, ch 7, starting in second chain from the hook, 6 sc in the back loops, 3 sc in the sts from R4, ch 7, starting in second chain from the hook, 6 sc in the back loops, 2 sc in the sts from R4 (18)

R6: 1 sc, 6 sc in the front loops of the chain, 9 sc, 6 sc in the front loops of the chain, 8 sc (30)

R7: 1 sc in each st (30)

Switch to Blood Orange yarn.

R8: 1 sc in each st (30)

R9: [8 sc, 1 dec] x3 (27)

Switch to Paper White yarn.

R10: 1 sc in each st (27)

R11: [7 sc, 1 dec] x3 (24)

Switch to Blood Orange yarn.

R12: Working through one fin and the body together, 2 sc, then 10 sc, working through the remaining fin and the body together, 2 sc, then 10 sc (24)

R13: [6 sc, 1 dec] x3 (21)

Switch to Paper White yarn.

R14: 1 sc in each st (21)

R15: [5 sc, 1 dec] x3 (18)

Switch to Blood Orange yarn.

R16: [4 sc, 1 dec] x3 (15)

R17: [3 sc, 1 dec] x3 (12)

Place the eyes between R14 and R15, on either side of the head. Stuff the piece with polyester fiberfill.

Switch to Paper White yarn.

R18: 6 dec (6)

R19–20: 1 sc in each st (6)

Close off, and then hide the yarn end with a tapestry needle.

Fish, round 6   *Fish, round 12*

A Little Dirt
Never Hurt

I haven't always had a green thumb; fake plants were my best friends for a while. But since meeting my husband, time spent outdoors with our plants and animals has become some of my most cherished moments. We have developed our property into somewhat of an urban homestead, complete with raised garden beds, fruit trees, chickens, a bunny, a tortoise and two dogs. Our home has been affectionately dubbed the Hu Zoo and is a well-loved attraction among our neighbors, friends and family. Every day is a learning process to get the soil, water, sun and nutrient conditions just right. But once we are more established, I hope to start a community harvest box where people can share extra produce, plants and seeds with their neighbors.

This chapter was inspired by our gardening and homesteading journey and is filled with the beautiful fruits, veggies and other plants we currently grow or hope to grow soon. But whether you garden or not, this chapter is full of fun and simple patterns for the fresh food lovers. Plus, with my no-sew techniques, you'll be able to whip up Tina the Turnip (page 49), Meyer the Lemon (page 63) or Gus the Mushroom (page 69) much faster than it takes to grow the real thing!

Skill Level: 3

Materials

0.5 oz Paintbox Yarns Cotton Aran in Pistachio (or similar worsted weight/aran yarn)

0.5 oz Paintbox Yarns Cotton Aran in Soft Fudge (or similar worsted weight/aran yarn)

1 oz Paintbox Yarns Cotton Aran in Paper White (or similar worsted weight/aran yarn)

Size E-4 (3.5-mm) crochet hook

Stitch marker for marking first st

2 (¼" [6-mm]) black plastic safety eyes

Scrap piece of black yarn for embroidery

Polyester fiberfill

Tapestry needle

Fern the Potted Plant

For the well-meaning plant killer, this is the pattern for you! Finally, an adorable little plant that won't wilt and die. Fern the Potted Plant is worked in continuous rounds and joins together with no sewing necessary. The leaves are made first and worked into the soil, then you'll switch to white yarn to create the pot, but feel free to change up the color to match your aesthetic! This pattern has a couple of components, including attaching the leaves and working through two rows together to create the lip of the pot, so it may take a bit longer on your first try. Fern's finished size is approximately 4 inches (10 cm) tall and 2½ inches (6.5 cm) wide.

Terminology

R1: row 1 or round 1

st(s): stitch(es)

ch: chain

slst: slip stitch

sc: single crochet

hdc: half double crochet

inc: single crochet increase

dec: invisible decrease

sc2tog: single crochet two together

MR: magic ring

FLO: front loops only

BLO: back loops only

Leaves

This piece starts at one end of the leaves, using Pistachio yarn.

Ch 19,

R1: Starting at the second chain from the hook, 18 sc (18)

R2: Ch 1, turn, [ch 9, starting at the second chain from the hook, 1 slst, 1 sc, 6 hdc, skip 1 sc of the foundation stitches, 1 slst in next foundation stitch] x9 to create a total of 9 leaves

Ch 1 and fasten off. There is no need to weave in the ends; the yarn will end up inside the piece.

(continued)

Pot

This piece starts with the soil, using Soft Fudge yarn.

R1: 6 sc in MR (6)

Hold the leaves and soil together as shown so that the leaves curl outward.

R2: Working through the foundation chain of the leaves and soil together, 1 inc in each st (12)

R3: Working through the foundation chain of the leaves and soil together, [1 sc, 1 inc] x6 (18)

R4: [2 sc, 1 inc] x6 (24)

Change to Paper White yarn.

R5: Working in FLO, 1 sc in each st (24)

R6: 1 sc in each st (24)

R7: Working in BLO, [3 sc, 1 inc] x6 (30)

R8: Working in BLO, 1 sc in each st (30)

R9: [3 sc, 1 dec] x6 (24)

Fold over the lip as shown.

R10: Working through the BLO of R9 and the BLO from R4 together, 1 sc in each st (24)

R11: [6 sc, 1 dec] x3 (21)

R12-13: 1 sc in each st (21)

R14: [5 sc, 1 dec] x3 (18)

R15-16: 1 sc in each st (18)

Place the eyes between R12 and R13, about 4 stitches apart. Using black yarn, embroider the mouth onto the front of the face, just below the eyes, using the tapestry needle. Stuff the piece with polyester fiberfill.

R17: Working in BLO, [1 sc, 1 sc2tog] x6 (12)

R18: 6 dec (6)

Close off, and then hide the yarn end with a tapestry needle.

Leaves, finished

Pot, rounds 2 and 3

Pot, round 10

Daisy the Flower

Although this chapter is mostly filled with fruits and veggies, flowers are a must in any garden. Not only are they a beautiful addition to your landscaping, but they also attract lots of beneficial bees. This pattern calls for white yarn, but feel free to try out your favorite colors and make a whole bouquet! Daisy the Flower is uniquely designed to be done quickly. The petals are made first and worked into the center of the flower to minimize sewing. Check out the Stitches and Techniques section (page 139) for tips on how to single crochet through multiple pieces. Daisy's finished size is approximately 4½ inches (11.5 cm) in diameter and 1½ inches (4 cm) thick.

Petals (x12)

This piece starts at the tip of each petal, using Paper White yarn.

R1: 6 sc in MR (6)

R2: [1 sc, 1 inc] x3 (9)

R3-4: 1 sc in each st (9)

R5: [1 sc, 1 dec] x3 (6)

R6: Ch 1, flatten the piece, then working through the front and backstitches together, 3 sc (3)

Ch 1 and fasten off. There is no need to weave in the ends; the yarn will end up inside the piece.

(continued)

Petals, round 6

Center

This piece starts at the center of the flower, using Daffodil Yellow yarn.

R1: 6 sc in MR (6)

R2: 1 inc in each st (12)

R3: [1 sc, 1 inc] x6 (18)

R4: [2 sc, 1 inc] x6 (24)

R5: [Working through one petal at a time and the center together, 3 sc, then 1 sc in next] x6 (24)

R6: 2 sc, [working through one petal at a time and the center together, 3 sc, then 1 sc in next] x5, then working through the last petal and the center together, 2 sc (24)

R7: Continue working through the last petal and the center together, 1sc, then 23 sc (24)

R8: [2 sc, 1 dec] x6 (18)

R9: [1 sc, 1 dec] x6 (12)

Place the eyes between R2 and R3, about 4 stitches apart. Using black yarn, embroider the mouth onto the front of the face, just below the eyes, using the tapestry needle. Stuff the piece with polyester fiberfill.

R10: 6 dec (6)

Close off, and then hide the yarn end with a tapestry needle.

Center, rounds 5 and 6

Daisy the Flower, finished

Terra the Shovel

No garden is complete without some tools to harvest your favorite veggies or dig a hole to plant some beautiful flowers. Getting your hands dirty is an absolute must for any garden lover. Terra the Shovel uses a slightly unique technique to create the base of the shovel's spade by working into the back loops of the chain, so you may want to set aside a little extra time for your first attempt. But once you get the hang of the pattern, I hope you dig it! Terra's finished size is approximately 6½ inches (16.5 cm) tall and 2 inches (5 cm) wide.

Shovel

The piece starts at the end of the handle, using Duck Egg Blue yarn.

R1: 6 sc in MR (6)

R2: 1 inc in each st (12)

R3: [3 sc, 1 inc] x3 (15)

R4-10: 1 sc in each st (15)

R11: 7 sc, place a stitch marker, 4 sc, place a stitch marker, 4 sc (15)

R12-15: 1 sc in each st (15)

Replace the stitch markers with safety eyes. Using black yarn, embroider the mouth onto the front of the face, just below the eyes, using the tapestry needle. Stuff the piece with polyester fiberfill.

R16: [3 sc, 1 dec] x3 (12)

R17: 6 dec (6)

Switch to Stormy Grey yarn.

R18: 1 sc in each st (6)

(continued)

R19: 3 sc, ch 4, starting in the second st, 3 sc in the back loops of the chain, 3 sc in sts from R15, ch 4, starting in the second st, 3 sc in the back loops of the chain (12)

R20: 3 sc, 3 sc in the front loops of the chain, 6 sc, 3 sc in the front loops of the chain, 3 sc (18)

R21-26: 1 sc in each st (18)

R27: [7 sc, 1 dec] x2 (16)

R28: [6 sc, 1 dec] x2 (14)

R29: [5 sc, 1 dec] x2 (12)

R30: [2 sc, 1 dec] x3 (9)

R31: [1 sc, 1 dec] x3 (6)

Do not stuff the spade of the shovel. Close off, cinching the last 6 sts tight, and then hide the yarn end with a tapestry needle.

Shovel, round 20

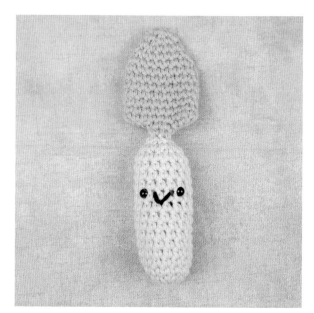

Terra the Shovel, finished

Tommy the Tomato

One of our most successful crops in our backyard garden is our little cherry tomato plant! We love to pop off a handful of tomatoes and enjoy them as we work around the garden. They make the perfect snack, fresh from the vine. While Tommy the Tomato isn't as tasty, he's a fun little project to keep your hands busy when you're not in the garden. Tommy is worked in continuous rounds and joins together with no sewing necessary. The fruit is made first, then the leaves are worked into the free loops to minimize sewing. Tommy's finished size is approximately 2½ inches (6.5 cm) tall and 2½ inches (6.5 cm) wide.

Tomato

This piece starts at the top of the tomato, using Grass Green yarn.

R1: 6 sc in MR (6)

Switch to Pillar Red yarn.

R2: Working in BLO, 1 inc in each st (12)

R3: [1 sc, 1 inc] x6 (18)

R4: [2 sc, 1 inc] x6 (24)

R5: [3 sc, 1 inc] x6 (30)

R6: [4 sc, 1 inc] x6 (36)

R7-9: 1 sc in each st (36)

Place the eyes between R8 and R9, about 4 stitches apart. Using black yarn, embroider the mouth onto the front of the face, just below the eyes, using the tapestry needle. Stuff the piece with polyester fiberfill.

(continued)

R10: [4 sc, 1 dec] x6 (30)

R11: [3 sc, 1 dec] x6 (24)

R12: [2 sc, 1 dec] x6 (18)

R13: [1 sc, 1 dec] x6 (12)

R14: 6 dec (6)

Close off, and then hide the yarn end with a tapestry needle.

Leaves

Using Grass Green yarn, join the yarn to the first front loop of R1 left behind from R2 of the tomato, ch 1, then start your first stitch in the same stitch as the join.

R1: Working into the FLO from R1, [(1 hdc, ch 2, 1 hdc, 1 slst) in the same stitch] x6 (30)

Slst in next st. Fasten off and weave in the ends with a tapestry needle.

Leaves, joining yarn

Leaves, finished

Tommy the Tomato, finished

Tina the Turnip

There's no denying, Tina the Turnip is simply the best. Her edible counterparts can be cooked, pickled or eaten raw, and the sharp taste of fresh turnips makes for a great addition to salads. Tina is worked in continuous rounds and joins together with no sewing necessary. The leaves are made first and worked into the turnip for a quick and fun pattern. These techniques may take some getting used to, so set aside some extra time for your first try. Tina's finished size is approximately 4 inches (10 cm) tall and 2 inches (5 cm) wide.

Leaves

This piece starts at one end of the leaves, using Pistachio yarn.

Ch 7,

R1: Starting at the second chain from the hook, 6 sc (6)

R2: Ch 1, turn, [ch 9, starting at the second chain from the hook, 1 sc, 1 hdc, 1 sc, 1 slst, 1 sc, 1 hdc, 1 sc, 1 slst, skip 1 sc of the foundation stitches, 1 slst in next foundation stitch] x3 to create a total of 3 leaves

Ch 1 and fasten off. There is no need to weave in the ends; the yarn will end up inside the piece.

(continued)

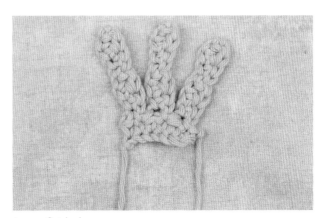

Leaves, finished

Turnip

This piece starts at the top of the turnip, using Pale Lilac yarn.

R1: 6 sc in MR (6)

Hold the leaves and turnip together as shown so that the leaves curl outward.

R2: Working through the foundation chain of the leaves and turnip together, 1 inc in each st (12)

R3: [1 sc, 1 inc] x6 (18)

R4: [2 sc, 1 inc] x6 (24)

R5: [3 sc, 1 inc] x6 (30)

R6-7: 1 sc in each st (30)

Switch to Paper White yarn.

R8-9: 1 sc in each st (30)

R10: [3 sc, 1 dec] x6 (24)

Place the eyes between R8 and R9, about 4 stitches apart. Using black yarn, embroider the mouth onto the front of the face with a tapestry needle, just below the eyes. Stuff the piece with polyester fiberfill.

R11: [2 sc, 1 dec] x6 (18)

R12: [1 sc, 1 dec] x6 (12)

R13: 6 dec (6)

Close off, leaving about a 1-inch (2.5-cm) tail.

Turnip, round 2

Tina the Turnip, finished

Skill Level: 1

Materials

0.5 oz Paintbox Yarns Cotton Aran in Soft Fudge (or similar worsted weight/aran yarn)

1 oz Paintbox Yarns Cotton Aran in Daffodil Yellow (or similar worsted weight/aran yarn)

Size E-4 (3.5-mm) crochet hook

Stitch marker for marking the first st

2 (¼" [6-mm]) black plastic safety eyes

Scrap piece of black yarn for embroidery

Polyester fiberfill

Tapestry needle

Terminology

R1: row 1 or round 1

st(s): stitch(es)

sc: single crochet

inc: single crochet increase

dec: invisible decrease

MR: magic ring

FLO: front loops only

BLO: back loops only

Blossom the Squash

Squashes are another one of our garden favorites! We are currently growing spaghetti squash, kabocha squash and pumpkins. Most of them accidentally started sprouting from our compost pile. Then, they got bigger, and the vines spread all through our garden. Our pet tortoise, named Turbo, loves to munch on the bright yellow blossoms! The flowers he doesn't eat eventually grow into big yellow squashes, just like Blossom the Squash. Blossom is a super quick and straightforward pattern, perfect for beginners. Blossom's finished size is approximately 4½ inches (11.5 cm) tall and 2½ inches (6.5 cm) wide.

Squash

This piece starts at the top of the stem, using Soft Fudge yarn.

R1: 6 sc in MR (6)

R2: Working in BLO, 1 sc in each st (6)

R3: 1 sc in each st (6)

Switch to Daffodil Yellow yarn.

R4: Working in FLO, 1 inc in each st (12)

R5: [1 sc, 1 inc] x6 (18)

R6–11: 1 sc in each st (18)

R12: [2 sc, 1 inc] x6 (24)

R13: [3 sc, 1 inc] x6 (30)

R14: [4 sc, 1 inc] x6 (36)

R15–18: 1 sc in each st (36)

(continued)

Place the eyes between R15 and R16, about 4 stitches apart. Using black yarn, embroider the mouth onto the front of the face, just below the eyes, using the tapestry needle.

R19: [4 sc, 1 dec] x6 (30)

R20: [3 sc, 1 dec] x6 (24)

R21: [2 sc, 1 dec] x6 (18)

R22: [1 sc, 1 dec] x6 (12)

Stuff the piece with polyester fiberfill.

R23: 6 dec (6)

Close off, and then hide the yarn end with a tapestry needle.

Blossom the Squash, finished

Carol the Carrot

Carrots are a great healthy snack, but I personally prefer them in cake form. I'm sure it completely negates the health benefits, but who can turn down a deliciously moist carrot cake with cinnamon, ginger and nutmeg, smothered in cream cheese frosting? Carol the Carrot is just as sweet as carrot cake, but she is worked in continuous rounds and joins together with no sewing necessary. The leaves are made first as one continuous piece and worked into the carrot to cut down on time. This technique is unique, so you may want to set aside some extra time for your first try. Carol's finished size is approximately 5½ inches (14 cm) tall and 1½ inches (4 cm) wide.

Leaves

This piece starts at one end of the leaves, using Pistachio yarn.

Ch 19,

R1: Starting at the second chain from the hook, 18 sc (18)

R2: Ch 1, turn, [ch 9, starting at the second chain from the hook, 1 slst, 1 sc, 6 hdc, skip 1 sc of the foundation stitches, 1 slst in next foundation stitch] x9 to create a total of 9 leaves

Ch 1 and fasten off. There is no need to weave in the ends; the yarn will end up inside the piece.

(continued)

Leaves, finished

Carrot

This piece starts at the top of the carrot using Blood Orange yarn.

R1: 6 sc in MR (6)

Hold the leaves and carrot together as shown so that the leaves curl outward.

R2: Working through the foundation chain of the leaves and carrot together, 1 inc in each st (12)

R3: Working through the foundation chain of the leaves and carrot together, [1 sc, 1 inc] x6 (18)

R4: [5 sc, 1 inc] x3 (21)

R5–7: 1 sc in each st (21)

R8: [5 sc, 1 dec] x3 (18)

R9: 1 sc in each st (18)

R10: [4 sc, 1 dec] x3 (15)

Place the eyes between R7 and R8, about 4 stitches apart. Using black yarn, embroider the mouth onto the front of the face, just below the eyes, using the tapestry needle.

R11: 1 sc in each st (15)

R12: [3 sc, 1 dec] x3 (12)

R13: 1 sc in each st (12)

Stuff the piece with polyester fiberfill.

R14: [2 sc, 1 dec] x3 (9)

R15: 1 sc in each st (9)

R16: [1 sc, 1 dec] x3 (6)

R17: 1 sc in each st (6)

Close off, and then hide the yarn end with a tapestry needle.

Carrot, rounds 2 and 3

Carol the Carrot, finished

Barry the Strawberry

Skill Level: 2

Materials

0.5 oz Paintbox Yarns Cotton Aran in Pistachio (or similar worsted weight/aran yarn)

0.5 oz Paintbox Yarns Cotton Aran in Pillar Red (or similar worsted weight/aran yarn)

0.5 oz Paintbox Yarns Cotton Aran in Paper White (or similar worsted weight/aran yarn)

Size E-4 (3.5-mm) crochet hook

Stitch marker for marking the first st

2 (¼" [6-mm]) black plastic safety eyes

Scrap piece of black yarn for embroidery

Polyester fiberfill

Tapestry needle

Strawberries are my all-time favorite fruit, so I definitely had to include a pattern here. Whether baked into pies or blended into a milk shake, I can't resist a strawberry! Barry the Strawberry is worked in continuous rounds, periodically working in a white stitch for the seeds. The fruit is made first, then the leaves are worked into the free loops to minimize sewing. Barry's finished size is approximately 2½ inches (6.5 cm) tall and 2 inches (5 cm) wide.

Terminology

R1: row 1 or round 1

st(s): stitch(es)

slst: slip stitch

ch: chain

sc: single crochet

inc: single crochet increase

dec: invisible decrease

hdc: half double crochet

MR: magic ring

BLO: back loops only

YO: yarn over

FLO: front loops only

Strawberry

This piece starts at the top of the strawberry, using Pistachio yarn.

R1: 6 sc in MR (6)

Switch to Pillar Red yarn. The remaining stitches will be worked in Pillar Red yarn unless specified otherwise. For the white stitches, stop when you have the last 2 red loops on your hook. With Paper White yarn, YO and pull the yarn through both loops. Insert your hook into the stitch. YO and draw up a loop. You should have 2 white loops on your hook. Switching back to Pillar Red yarn, YO again and pull the yarn through both loops. There is no need to cut the old color and tie the ends together; just drop the yarn inside the piece when it is not being used, and pick up the yarn again for the next white stitch.

R2: Working in BLO, 1 inc in each st (12)

R3: [1 sc, 1 inc] x6 (18)

Color change

(continued)

R4: [2 sc, 1 inc, 1 sc, 1 sc in white, 1 inc] x3 (24)

R5: [3 sc, 1 inc] x6 (30)

R6: [1 sc in white, 9 sc] x3 (30)

R7: [8 sc, 1 dec] x3 (27)

R8: [4 sc, 1 sc in white, 2 sc, 1 dec] x3 (24)

R9: [6 sc, 1 dec] x3 (21)

R10: [1 sc in white, 4 sc, 1 dec] x3 (18)

R11: [4 sc, 1 dec] x3 (15)

Place the eyes between R8 and R9, about 4 stitches apart. Using black yarn, embroider the mouth onto the front of the face, just below the eyes, using the tapestry needle. Stuff the piece with polyester fiberfill.

R12: [2 sc, 1 sc in white, 1 dec] x3 (12)

R13: 6 dec (6)

Close off and hide the yarn end with a tapestry needle.

Leaves

Using Pistachio yarn, join the yarn to the first front loop of R1 left behind from R2 of the strawberry, ch 1, then start your first stitch in the same stitch as the join.

R1: Working into the FLO from R1, [(1 hdc, ch 2, 1 hdc, 1 slst) in the same stitch] x6 (30)

Slst in next st. Fasten off and weave in the ends with a tapestry needle.

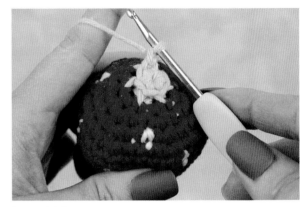

Leaves, joining yarn

Leaves, finished

Barry the Strawberry, finished

Bart the Pear

The pear tree in our backyard is still quite small, so we're only getting a handful of pears right now. But once we have enough, my husband makes spiced-pear jam that is to die for. On lazy Sunday mornings, we'll sometimes make waffles and eat them with homemade pear jam, whipped cream and fresh fruit. That tradition inspired this super beginner-friendly pattern that can be worked up quickly without any special techniques or tricks. Bart the Pear's finished size is approximately 3½ inches (9 cm) tall and 2½ inches (6.5 cm) wide.

Pear

This piece starts at the top of the stem, using Soft Fudge yarn.

R1: 4 sc in MR (4)

R2: Working in BLO, [1 sc, 1 inc] x2 (6)

R3: 1 sc in each st (6)

Switch to Pistachio yarn.

R4: Working in FLO, 1 inc in each st (12)

R5: [1 sc, 1 inc] x6 (18)

R6: [5 sc, 1 inc] x3 (21)

R7: [6 sc, 1 inc] x3 (24)

R8-10: 1 sc in each st (24)

R11: [3 sc, 1 inc] x6 (30)

R12: [4 sc, 1 inc] x6 (36)

R13-17: 1 sc in each st (36)

(continued)

Place the eyes between R14 and R15, about 4 stitches apart. Using black yarn, embroider the mouth onto the front of the face, just below the eyes, using the tapestry needle.

R18: [4 sc, 1 dec] x6 (30)

R19: [3 sc, 1 dec] x6 (24)

R20: [2 sc, 1 dec] x6 (18)

R21: [1 sc, 1 dec] x6 (12)

Stuff the piece with polyester fiberfill.

R22: dec (6)

Close off, and then hide the yarn end with a tapestry needle.

Bart the Pear, finished

Meyer the Lemon

When we moved in, our house already had an established lemon tree that provides more lemons than we can handle! We make lemonade, lemon bars, lemon cake and anything else we can think of. Once our community harvest box is set up, which is a goal of ours once our backyard garden is producing enough, we will definitely load it up with all the extra lemons from our tree. For now, Meyer the Lemon will serve as a cute little reminder to achieve our goals! Meyer is worked in continuous rounds and uses a special technique to transition to the lemon rind that requires working through two rows together, so your first attempt might take some extra time. Meyer's finished size is approximately 2½ inches (6.5 cm) tall and 2½ inches (6.5 cm) wide.

Lemon

This piece starts at the center of the lemon, using Paper White yarn.

R1: 6 sc in MR (6)

Switch to Daffodil Yellow yarn.

R2: 1 inc in each st (12)

R3: [1 sc, 1 inc] x6 (18)

R4: [2 sc, 1 inc] x6 (24)

Switch to Paper White yarn.

R5: [3 sc, 1 inc] x6 (30)

Switch to Buttercup Yellow yarn.

(continued)

R6: Working in FLO, [1 inc, 4 sc] x6 (36)

R7: Working in BLO, [4 sc, 1 sc2tog] x6 (30)

Fold over the lip as shown.

R8: Working through R7 and the BLO of R5 together, 1 sc in each st (30)

R9–11: 1 sc in each st (30)

Place the eyes between R2 and R3, about 4 stitches apart. Using black yarn, embroider the mouth onto the front of the face, just below the eyes, using the tapestry needle. Use Paper White yarn and a tapestry needle to embroider lines along the face of the lemon as shown.

R12: [8 sc, 1 dec] x3 (27)

R13: [7 sc, 1 dec] x3 (24)

R14: [2 sc, 1 dec] x6 (18)

R15: [1 sc, 1 dec] x6 (12)

Stuff the piece with polyester fiberfill.

R16: 6 dec (6)

R17: 1 sc in each st (6)

Close off, and then hide the yarn end with a tapestry needle.

Lemon, round 8 (with the lip folded over)

Meyer the Lemon, finished

Cheyenne the Cayenne Pepper

Skill Level: 1

Materials

0.5 oz Paintbox Yarns Cotton Aran in Pillar Red (or similar worsted weight/ aran yarn)

0.5 oz Paintbox Yarns Cotton Aran in Grass Green (or similar worsted weight/ aran yarn)

Size E-4 (3.5-mm) crochet hook

Stitch marker for marking the first st

2 (¼" [6-mm]) black plastic safety eyes

Scrap piece of black yarn for embroidery

Polyester fiberfill

Tapestry needle

Terminology

R1: row 1 or round 1

st(s): stitch(es)

sc: single crochet

inc: single crochet increase

dec: invisible decrease

MR: magic ring

FLO: front loops only

Personally, I max out at about a 5 out of 10 on the spice scale. Any more than that, and I'll start sweating and crying, but my husband loves spicy foods! So, I made this pattern just for him. Cheyenne the Cayenne Pepper is a fun and simple project that comes together in no time to add a little spice to your life. The pattern is worked in continuous rounds with a few strategically placed increases and decreases to create its classic shape. Cheyenne's finished size is approximately 4 inches (10 cm) tall and 1½ inches (4 cm) wide.

Pepper

This piece starts at the bottom of the pepper, using Pillar Red yarn.

R1: 6 sc in MR (6)

R2: 5 sc, 1 inc (7)

R3: 6 sc, 1 inc (8)

R4: 7 sc, 1 inc (9)

R5: 8 sc, 1 inc (10)

R6: 9 sc, 1 inc (11)

R7: 10 sc, 1 inc (12)

R8: 10 sc, 2 inc (14)

R9: 11 sc, 1 inc, 1 sc, 1 inc (16)

R10: 12 sc, 1 inc, 2 sc, 1 inc (18)

(continued)

R 11–14: 1 sc in each st (18)

Place the eyes between R11 and R12, about 4 stitches apart. Using black yarn, embroider the mouth onto the front of the face, just below the eyes, using the tapestry needle.

R 15: [1 sc, 1 dec] x6 (12)

Stuff the piece with polyester fiberfill.

R 16: 6 dec (6)

Switch to Grass Green yarn.

R 17: Working in FLO, 1 sc in each st (6)

R 18: [1 sc, 1 dec] x2 (4)

Close off, and then hide the yarn end with a tapestry needle.

Cheyenne the Cayenne Pepper, finished

Materials

0.5 oz Paintbox Yarns
Cotton Aran in Pillar Red
(or similar worsted weight/
aran yarn)

0.5 oz Paintbox Yarns
Cotton Aran in Paper White
(or similar worsted weight/
aran yarn)

Size E-4 (3.5-mm) crochet
hook

Stitch marker for marking
the first st

2 (¼" [6-mm]) black plastic
safety eyes

Scrap piece of black yarn
for embroidery

Polyester fiberfill

Tapestry needle

Terminology

R1: row 1 or round 1

st(s): stitch(es)

slst: slip stitch

sc: single crochet

inc: single crochet increase

dec: invisible decrease

sc2tog: single crochet two
together

MR: magic ring

FLO: front loops only

BLO: back loops only

YO: yarn over

Gus the Mushroom

If we were to grow mushrooms in our garden, I would love to include button mushrooms for my pizza, enoki mushrooms for my hot pot and pretty much any mushroom to use in pasta. Unfortunately, I'm pretty sure red and white fungi, like Gus the Mushroom, are poisonous so we can't eat those—but we can crochet them! Gus the Mushroom is worked in continuous rounds, periodically working in a white stitch throughout. The mushroom cap is made first, then the stump is worked into the free loops to minimize sewing. Attaching the stump and the repeating color changes make this pattern a little trickier and may take some practice. Gus's finished size is approximately 3 inches (7.5 cm) tall and 2 inches (5 cm) wide.

Mushroom Top

This piece starts at the top of the mushroom, using Pillar Red yarn.

These stitches will be worked in Pillar Red yarn unless specified otherwise. For the white stitches, stop when you have the last 2 red loops on your hook. With Paper White yarn, YO and pull the yarn through both loops on the hook. Insert your hook into the stitch. YO and draw up a loop. You should have 2 white loops on your hook. Switching back to Pillar Red yarn, YO again and pull the yarn through both loops on the hook. There is no need to cut the old color and tie the ends together inside the piece; just drop the yarn inside the piece when it is not being used, and pick up the yarn again for the next white stitch.

(continued)

Color change

R1: 6 sc in MR (6)

R2: 1 inc in each st (12)

R3: [1 sc, 1 inc, 1 sc in white, 1 inc] x3 (18)

R4: [2 sc, 1 inc] x6 (24)

R5: [1 sc in white, 2 sc, 1 inc, 3 sc, 1 inc] x3 (30)

R6: 1 sc in each st (30)

R7: [3 sc, 1 sc in white, 6 sc] x3 (30)

R8: 1 sc in each st (30)

R9: [8 sc, 1 sc in white, 1 sc] x3 (30)

R10: Working in FLO, 1 sc in each st (30)

Slst in next st. Fasten off and weave in the ends with a tapestry needle.

Place the eyes between R7 and R8, about 4 stitches apart. Using black yarn, embroider the mouth onto the front of the face, just below the eyes, using the tapestry needle.

Mushroom Stump

Using Paper White yarn, join the yarn to the first back loop of R9 left behind from R10 of the mushroom cap, ch 1, then start your first stitch in the same stitch as the join.

R1: Working into the BLO of R9, [3 sc, sc2tog] x6 (24)

R2: [2 sc, 1 dec] x6 (18)

R3: [1 sc, 1 dec] x6 (12)

R4: Working in FLO, 1 sc in each st (12)

R5: [3 sc, 1 inc] x3 (15)

R6: 1 sc in each st (15)

R7: [4 sc, 1 inc] x3 (18)

R8: [1 sc, 1 dec] x6 (12)

Stuff the piece with polyester fiberfill.

R9: 6 dec (6)

Close off, and then hide the yarn end with a tapestry needle.

Mushroom stump, joining yarn

Gus the Mushroom, finished

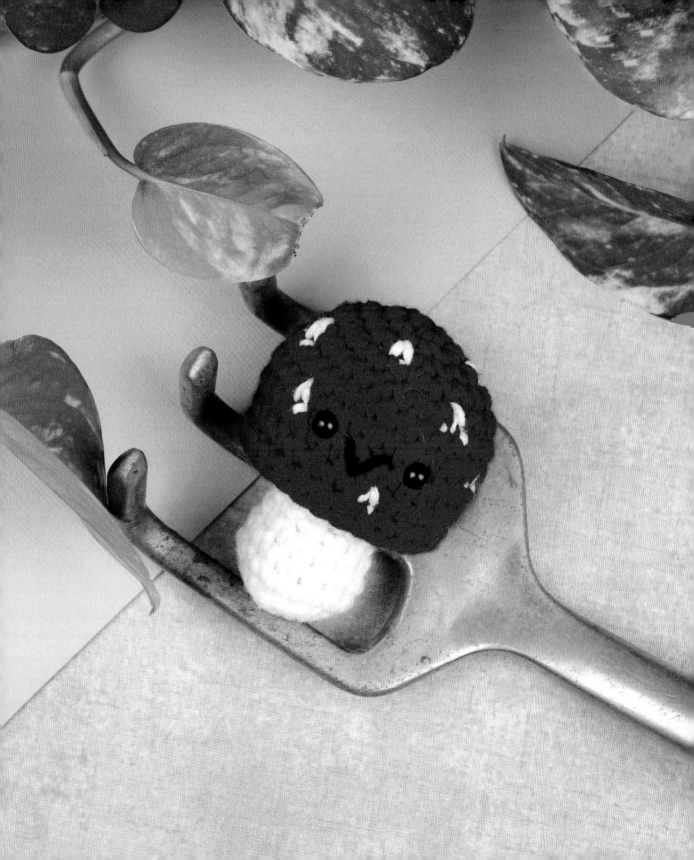

What's Cookin', Good Lookin'?

At home, we love to host gatherings with our friends and family and always prepare a feast! Portioning and planning go out the window and we inevitably end up cooking enough to feed an army. My husband will make delicious burgers or smoked meats, and I'll be in charge of the sides and baked goods.

So, I filled this chapter with some cooking basics to help you get your very own crochet kitchen up and running. I've got you covered, whether you need ketchup and mustard for your burgers (page 93), seasoning for steaks (page 91) or eggs (page 81) and a rolling pin (page 82) to make a pie. Nothing brings people together quite like food, especially when you're spending time in the kitchen and preparing a meal.

This chapter is centered on kitchen and pantry staples, but if you're looking for more food designs, check out my previous book, *Hooked on Amigurumi*. Its "Eat Your Heart Out" chapter includes more fun patterns, including jars of peanut butter and jelly, a cherry pie and even a chicken drumstick! With these two chapters together, you'll have a fully stocked crochet kitchen for you or your little one. I'll be sure to get you set up in no time with these fun and simple no-sew patterns. So let's get cookin', good lookin'!

Materials

1 oz Paintbox Yarns Cotton Aran in Pillar Red (or similar worsted weight/aran yarn)

Size E-4 (3.5-mm) crochet hook

Stitch marker for marking the first st

2 (¼" [6-mm]) black plastic safety eyes

Scrap piece of black yarn for embroidery

Polyester fiberfill

Tapestry needle

Terminology

R1: row 1 or round 1

st(s): stitch(es)

ch: chain

slst: slip stitch

sc: single crochet

inc: single crochet increase

dec: invisible decrease

MR: magic ring

Mitsy the Oven Mitt

In a pinch, sometimes I'll just pull the sleeves of my sweater over my hands to grab a hot pan. But I'll be the first to admit, oven mitts would definitely be a smarter and safer choice. Mitsy the Oven Mitt still won't be able to help you when you're making a casserole, baking cookies or roasting a chicken, but at least she's cute! Mitsy is worked in continuous rounds. The thumb and mitt are made first and then joined together to create a seamless piece, which may take some practice. Mitsy's finished size is approximately 4 inches (10 cm) tall and 3 inches (7.5 cm) wide.

Thumb

This piece starts at the top of the thumb, using Pillar Red yarn.

R1: 6 sc in MR (6)

R2: [1 sc, 1 inc] x3 (9)

R3–5: 1 sc in each st (9)

Slst in next st and fasten off. There is no need to weave in the ends; the yarn will end up inside the piece.

Mitt

This piece starts at the top of the mitt, using Pillar Red yarn.

R1: 6 sc in MR (6)

R2: 1 inc in each st (12)

R3: [1 sc, 1 inc] x6 (18)

R4: [2 sc, 1 inc] x6 (24)

R5–11: 1 sc in each st (24)

(continued)

Leaving your hook in the last stitch, continue to the next piece.

Palm

Hold the thumb and palm together as shown. With the last loop of the mitt still on your hook, slst 1 through both pieces to join. For the next round, crochet clockwise around both pieces, excluding the slst used to join.

R1: 23 sc around the mitt, 8 sc around the thumb (31)

R2: 1 dec, 19 sc, 2 dec, 4 sc, 1 dec (27)

R3: 1 dec, 17 sc, 2 dec, 2 sc, 1 dec (23)

R4–5: 1 sc in each st (23)

R6: 10 sc, 1 dec, 11 sc (22)

Place the eyes between R2 and R3, about 4 stitches apart. Using black yarn, embroider the mouth onto the front of the face, just below the eyes, using the tapestry needle.

After R6, work about 10 sc so you're at the side of the mitt. Stuff the piece with polyester fiberfill.

R7: Ch 1, flatten the piece, then working through front and backstitches together, sc 11 (11)

R8: Ch 1, turn, 1 sc in each st (11)

Ch 1 then fasten off. Leave a loop on the end as shown and weave in the ends.

Palm, joining

Palm, round 7

Mitsy the Oven Mitt, finished

Materials

1 oz Paintbox Yarns Cotton Aran in Duck Egg Blue (or similar worsted weight/aran yarn)

Size E-4 (3.5-mm) crochet hook

Stitch marker for marking the first st

2 (¼" [6-mm]) black plastic safety eyes

Scrap piece of black yarn for embroidery

Polyester fiberfill

Tapestry needle

Terminology

R1: row 1 or round 1

st(s): stitch(es)

ch: chain

slst: slip stitch

sc: single crochet

inc: single crochet increase

dec: invisible decrease

sc2tog: single crochet two together

MR: magic ring

FLO: front loops only

BLO: back loops only

Stark the Stockpot

Whenever I'm feeling ill, my husband always makes me a steaming bowl of chicken soup from scratch. It never fails to warm my soul and give me life! I'm so grateful to have such a caring husband—and, of course, a sturdy stockpot for making the soup! Stark the Stockpot is worked in continuous rounds with no sewing necessary. The handles are made first and worked into the pot, then the brim is added to the free loops. These techniques may be a bit tricky at first, so set aside some extra time, if needed. Stark's finished size is approximately 3½ inches (9 cm) tall and 3 inches (7.5 cm) wide.

Handles (x2)

This piece starts at the edge of the handle, using Duck Egg Blue yarn to create an oval.

Ch 4,

R1: Then starting at the second chain from the hook, sc 3 in the back loops, rotate the chain, then sc 3 in the front loops (6)

R2: Ch 1, flatten the piece, then working through the front and backstitches together, sc 3 (3)

Ch 1 and fasten off. There is no need to weave in the ends; the yarn will end up inside the piece.

(continued)

Handles, finished

Pot

This piece starts at the top of the lid, using Duck Egg Blue yarn.

R1: 6 sc in MR (6)

R2: 1 sc in each st (6)

R3: Working in FLO, 1 inc in each st (12)

R4: [1 sc, 1 inc] x6 (18)

R5: [2 sc, 1 inc] x6 (24)

R6: [3 sc, 1 inc] x6 (30)

R7: [4 sc, 1 inc] x6 (36)

R8: [5 sc, 1 inc] x6 (42)

R9: Working in BLO, 1 sc in each st (42)

R10: [18 sc, then, working through the handle and the pot together, 3 sc] x2 (42)

R11: [12 sc, 1 dec] x3 (39)

R12-13: 1 sc in each st (39)

R14: [11 sc, 1 dec] x3 (36)

R15-16: 1 sc in each st (36)

Place the eyes between R12 and R13, about 4 stitches apart. Using black yarn, embroider the mouth onto the front of the face, just below the eyes, using the tapestry needle.

R17: Working in BLO, [4 sc, 1 sc2tog] x6 (30)

R18: [3 sc, 1 dec] x6 (24)

R19: [2 sc, 1 dec] x6 (18)

R20: [1 sc, 1 dec] x6 (12)

Stuff the piece with polyester fiberfill.

R21: 6 dec (6)

Close off, and then hide the yarn end with a tapestry needle.

Brim

Using Duck Egg Blue yarn, join the yarn to the first front loop from R8 left behind from R9 of the pot, ch 1, then start your first stitch in the same stitch as the join.

R1: Working FLO from R8, [6 sc, 1 inc] x6 (48)

Slst in next st. Fasten off and weave in the ends with a tapestry needle.

Pot, round 10   *Brim, joining yarn*

Stark the Stockpot, finished

Gregg the Egg

My husband and I recently started raising backyard chickens! The ladies currently lay about six eggs a day in a variety of beautiful colors. They are perfect for morning breakfast or baking, or to top off a burger. Don't tell the other chickens, but my favorite hen is our Buff Orpington named Kate, who lays beautiful pale pink eggs. This pattern is quick, easy and extremely beginner-friendly. You may even be able to crochet a half dozen in one sitting and create a rainbow of eggs to match my hens! Gregg's finished size is approximately 2½ inches (6.5 cm) tall and 2 inches (5 cm) wide.

Egg

This piece starts at the top of the egg, using any color yarn.

R1: 6 sc in MR (6)

R2: 1 inc in each st (12)

R3: [3 sc, 1 inc] x3 (15)

R4: [4 sc, 1 inc] x3 (18)

R5: [5 sc, 1 inc] x3 (21)

R6: [6 sc, 1 inc] x3 (24)

R7-11: 1 sc in each st (24)

Place the eyes between R8 and R9, about 4 stitches apart. Using black yarn, embroider the mouth onto the front of the face, just below the eyes, using the tapestry needle. Stuff the piece with polyester fiberfill.

R12: [2 sc, 1 dec] x6 (18)

R13: [1 sc, 1 dec] x6 (12)

R14: 6 dec (6)

Close off, and then hide the yarn end with a tapestry needle.

Julia the Rolling Pin

The name of this pattern was inspired by the iconic Julia Child, who said, "A party without cake is just a meeting." So, indulge! Whether your vice is piecrusts, pastry shells or pizza dough, Julia the Rolling Pin will get the job done. My personal preference is cookies! Julia the Rolling Pin is worked in continuous rounds to create an effortlessly seamless piece. This pattern just calls for a few rounds, working in the back or front loops only to create its shape. Julia's finished size is approximately 1½ inches (4 cm) tall and 6 inches (15 cm) long.

Rolling Pin

This piece starts at one end of the rolling pin, using Soft Fudge yarn. Stuff the piece with polyester fiberfill throughout.

R1: 6 sc in MR (6)

R2: 1 inc in each st (12)

R3: 1 sc in each st (12)

R4: [2 sc, 1 dec] x3 (9)

R5: [1 sc, 1 dec] x3 (6)

R6: 1 sc in each st (6)

R7: Working in FLO, 1 inc in each st (12)

R8: [3 sc, 1 inc] x3 (15)

R9: Working in BLO, 1 sc in each st (15)

R10-22: 1 sc in each st (15)

Place one eye between R13 and R14 and the second eye between R18 and R19. Using black yarn, embroider the mouth onto the front of the face, just below the eyes, using the tapestry needle.

(continued)

R23: Working in BLO, [3 sc, 1 sc2tog] x3 (12)

R24: 6 dec (6)

R25: Working in FLO, 1 sc in each st (6)

R26: [1 sc, 1 inc] x3 (9)

R27: [2 sc, 1 inc] x3 (12)

R28: 1 sc in each st (12)

R29: 6 dec (6)

Close off, and then hide the yarn end with a tapestry needle.

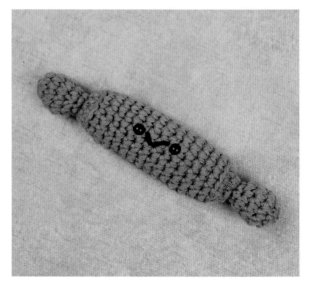

Julia the Rolling Pin, finished

Kerry the Butter

I remember as a kid, shaking up a jar of heavy cream for what felt like forever to make homemade butter. Then, we spread it over a slice of toast and it somehow tasted so delicious knowing we had made it ourselves. Butter truly makes everything better. Kerry the Butter is worked in two pieces: a stick of butter and a little extra pat of butter to put on Todd the Toast from *Hooked on Amigurumi*. Kerry's finished size is approximately 3 inches (7.5 cm) long and 1½ inches (4 cm) wide, and the pat of butter is approximately ½ inch (1.5 cm) thick and 1½ inches (4 cm) wide.

Pat of Butter

This piece starts at the center of the pat of butter, using Daffodil Yellow yarn.

R1: 4 sc in MR (4)

R2: 3 sc in each st (12)

R3: [1 sc, 3 sc in next, 1 sc] x4 (20)

R4: Working in BLO, 1 sc in each st (20)

R5: Working in BLO, [1 sc, sc3tog, 1 sc in next] x4 (12)

R6: [sc3tog] x4 (4)

Close off, and then hide the yarn end with a tapestry needle.

Stick of Butter

This piece starts at the center of the stick of butter, using Daffodil Yellow yarn.

R1: 4 sc in MR (4)

R2: 3 sc in each st (12)

R3: [1 sc, 3 sc in next, 1 sc] x4 (20)

R4: Working in BLO, 1 sc in each, placing a stitch marker in the last stitch (20)

(continued)

Place the eyes between R2 and R3. Using black yarn, embroider the mouth onto the front of the face, just below the eyes, using the tapestry needle.

R5–15: 1 sc in each

After R15, work about 2 sc so you're lined up with the stitch marker. Stuff the piece with polyester fiberfill.

R16: Working in BLO, [1 sc, sc3tog, 1 sc in next] x4 (12)

R17: [sc3tog] x4 (4)

Close off, and then hide the yarn end with a tapestry needle.

Kerry the Butter, finished

Bessie the Milk Jug

If I could, I would love to own cows for fresh milk! Bessie the Milk Jug uses a trick of working 3 sc at the corners to create a square shape. Her finished size is approximately 4½ inches (11.5 cm) tall and 2 inches (5 cm) wide.

Milk

This piece starts at the top of the milk jug, using Duck Egg Blue yarn.

R1: 6 sc in MR (6)

R2: 1 inc in each st (12)

R3: [1 sc, 1 inc] x6 (18)

R4: Working in BLO, 1 sc in each st (18)

R5: Working in BLO, [1 sc, 1 sc2tog] x6 (12)

Switch to Paper White yarn.

R6: [1 sc, 3 sc in next, 1 sc] x4 (20)

R7: [2 sc, 3 sc in next, 2 sc] x4, placing a stitch marker in the last stitch (28)

R8-10: 1 sc in each st (28)

Switch to Duck Egg Blue yarn.

R11-15: 1 sc in each st (28)

Switch to Paper White yarn.

R16-20: 1 sc in each st (28)

Place the eyes between R13 and R14, about 4 stitches apart. Using black yarn, embroider the mouth onto the front of the face, just below the eyes, using the tapestry needle. After R20, work about 2 sc so you're lined up with the stitch marker. Stuff the piece with polyester fiberfill.

R21: Working in BLO, [2 sc, sc3tog, 2 sc] x4 (20)

R22: [1 sc, sc3tog, 1 sc] x4 (12)

R23: [sc3tog] x4 (4)

Close off, and then hide the yarn end with a tapestry needle.

Skill Level: 1

Materials

0.5 oz Paintbox Yarns Cotton Aran in Stormy Grey (or similar worsted weight/aran yarn)

0.5 oz Paintbox Yarns Cotton Aran in Paper White (or similar worsted weight/aran yarn)

Size E-4 (3.5-mm) crochet hook

Stitch marker for marking the first st

2 (¼" [6-mm]) black plastic safety eyes

Scrap piece of black yarn for embroidery

Polyester fiberfill

Tapestry needle

Terminology

R1: row 1 or round 1

st(s): stitch(es)

sc: single crochet

inc: single crochet increase

dec: invisible decrease

sc2tog: single crochet two together

MR: magic ring

FLO: front loops only

BLO: back loops only

Morton the Salt Shaker

My husband's latest endeavor has been cooking smoked chickens, briskets, ribs and more. For the chickens, he brines them in salt for a day before cooking them in the smoker for a few hours, and it is a game changer! It's always incredibly delicious and moist. We go through so much salt and chicken each month, but I promise, I won't let him touch our pet chickens! Morton the Salt Shaker is a great beginner-friendly pattern that can be customized for your favorite seasonings. Try replacing the white yarn with dark grey for pepper, or red for paprika! Morton's finished size is approximately 3½ inches (9 cm) tall and 2 inches (5 cm) wide.

Salt Shaker

This piece starts at the top of the cap, using Stormy Grey yarn.

R1: 6 sc in MR (6)

R2: 1 inc in each st (12)

R3: [1 sc, 1 inc] x6 (18)

R4: 1 sc in each st (18)

R5: [1 sc, 1 dec] x6 (12)

R6: Working in BLO, 1 sc in each st (12)

R7: Working in BLO, 1 sc in each st (12)

Switch to Paper White yarn.

(continued)

R8: [3 sc, 1 inc] x3 (15)

R9: 1 sc in each st (15)

R10: [4 sc, 1 inc] x3 (18)

R11: 1 sc in each st (18)

R12: [5 sc, 1 inc] x3 (21)

R13: 1 sc in each st (21)

R14: [6 sc, 1 inc] x3 (24)

R15–17: 1 sc in each st (24)

Morton the Salt Shaker, finished

Place the eyes between R13 and R14, about 4 stitches apart. Using black yarn, embroider the mouth onto the front of the face, just below the eyes, using the tapestry needle. Stuff the piece with polyester fiberfill.

R18: Working in BLO, [2 sc, 1 sc2tog] x6 (18)

R19: [1 sc, 1 dec] x6 (12)

R20: 6 dec (6)

Close off, and then hide the yarn end with a tapestry needle.

Materials

1 oz Paintbox Yarns Cotton Aran in Pillar Red (or similar worsted weight/aran yarn)

1 oz Paintbox Yarns Cotton Aran in Buttercup Yellow (or similar worsted weight/aran yarn)

Size E-4 (3.5-mm) crochet hook

Stitch marker for marking the first st

2 (¼" [6-mm]) black plastic safety eyes

Scrap piece of black yarn for embroidery

Polyester fiberfill

Tapestry needle

Terminology

R1: row 1 or round 1

st(s): stitch(es)

sc: single crochet

inc: single crochet increase

dec: invisible decrease

sc2tog: single crochet two together

MR: magic ring

FLO: front loops only

BLO: back loops only

Hunt and Dijon the Ketchup and Mustard Bottles

This iconic pair has become a staple in American cuisine. Ketchup and mustard are a must for any barbecue, ball game or fast food run and are best served smothered over your hot dogs and hamburgers. This pattern calls for a few rounds working in the back or front loops only to create its shape. But Hunt and Dijon both follow the same fun and easy, beginner-friendly pattern. Alternatively, you can swap out the red and yellow yarn to make your favorite condiments! Hunt's and Dijon's finished size is approximately 4½ inches (11.5 cm) tall and 2 inches (5 cm) wide.

Bottles (x2)

This piece starts at the top of the bottle, using Pillar Red or Buttercup Yellow yarn.

R1: 4 sc in MR (4)

R2: Working in BLO, [1 sc, 1 inc] x2 (6)

R3–4: 1 sc in each st (6)

R5: Working in FLO, 1 inc in each st (12)

R6: [1 sc, 1 inc] x6 (18)

R7: Working in BLO, 1 sc in each st (18)

R8: 1 sc in each st (18)

R9: Working in FLO, [2 sc, 1 inc] x6 (24)

R10: Working in BLO, 1 sc in each st (24)

R11–22: 1 sc in each st (24)

(continued)

Place the eyes between R17 and R18, about 4 stitches apart. Using black yarn, embroider the mouth onto the front of the face, just below the eyes, using the tapestry needle. Stuff the piece with polyester fiberfill.

R23: Working in BLO, [2 sc, 1 sc2tog] x6 (18)

R24: [1 sc, 1 dec] x6 (12)

R25: 6 dec (6)

Close off, and then hide the yarn end with a tapestry needle.

Hunt and Dijon the Ketchup and Mustard Bottles, finished

the Season

I grew up celebrating every holiday, big and small. Each celebration was just an excuse to bring family together and eat delicious food. It was cheesy at times, but as each year passes, I cherish more and more these moments we spend together. Now, many of the parties have moved to our house and we have twice the guests as we join our two families! My husband and I cook up a storm while the adults are off drinking wine, and the dogs are running around the backyard chasing the nieces and nephews. As crazy and hectic as it is, my heart is so full after having the house filled with all that laughter and joy. I can't wait to carry on the tradition with our own children one day.

This chapter encapsulates those beautiful moments together celebrating each day and cherishing family and tradition. We have Dom the Champagne Bottle (page 99) for New Year's, Patch the Pumpkin (page 107) for Halloween, Jack the Snowman (page 120) for Christmas and many more! Plus, these patterns can be whipped up quickly in about an hour or less, so they make the perfect last-minute gift for any celebration!

Dom the Champagne Bottle

Whether you're celebrating the New Year, a special occasion or just grabbing brunch with friends, champagne is always a good idea. So, let's pop, fizz, clink and start off this chapter with a bottle of bubbly! This simple level 1 pattern is worked in continuous rounds and uses a series of color changes to create this classic look. You could also switch the colors and make your favorite bottle of wine, if you like. Dom's finished size is approximately 5½ inches (14 cm) tall and 2 inches (5 cm) wide.

Champagne Bottle

This piece starts at the top of the bottle, using Buttercup Yellow yarn.

R1: 6 sc in MR (6)

R2: 1 inc in each st (12)

R3: [1 sc, 1 inc] x6 (18)

R4: 1 sc in each st (18)

R5: [1 sc, 1 dec] x6 (12)

R6-9: 1 sc in each st (12)

Switch to Grass Green yarn.

R10: 1 sc in each st (12)

R11: [3 sc, 1 inc] x3 (15)

R12: [4 sc, 1 inc] x3 (18)

R13: [5 sc, 1 inc] x3 (21)

R14: [6 sc, 1 inc] x3 (24)

R15-16: 1 sc in each st (24)

(continued)

Switch to Paper White yarn.

R 17–21: 1 sc in each st (24)

Switch to Grass Green yarn.

R22–25: 1 sc in each st (24)

Place the eyes between R19 and R20, about 4 stitches apart. Using black yarn, embroider the mouth onto the front of the face, just below the eyes, using a tapestry needle. Stuff the piece with polyester fiberfill.

R26: Working in BLO, [2 sc, 1 sc2tog] x6 (18)

R27 : [1 sc, 1 dec] x6 (12)

R28: 6 dec (6)

Close off, and then hide the yarn end with a tapestry needle.

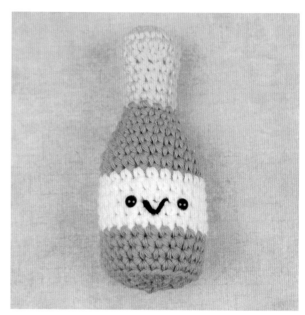

Dom the Champagne Bottle, finished

Skill Level: 2

Materials

1 oz Paintbox Yarns Cotton Aran in Pillar Red (or similar worsted weight/aran yarn)

Size E-4 (3.5-mm) crochet hook

Stitch marker for marking the first st

2 (¼" [6-mm]) black plastic safety eyes

Scrap piece of black yarn for embroidery

Polyester fiberfill

Tapestry needle

Terminology

R1: row 1 or round 1

st(s): stitch(es)

slst: slip stitch

sc: single crochet

inc: single crochet increase

dec: invisible decrease

MR: magic ring

Valentina the Heart

The day after Valentine's Day, many years ago, my now husband took me to Catalina Island for a fun little date. We had a great time snorkeling, eating and exploring the island. Then, we kayaked to a private beach, where he asked me to be his girlfriend! Since then, Valentine's Day has always held a special place in my heart, and Valentina the Heart is the perfect pattern for the occasion. She is worked in continuous rounds, starting with the two humps. Then, we use a sometimes-tricky technique to join the humps together and create a seamless, no-sew piece. Valentina's finished size is about 3 inches (7.5 cm) tall and 3 inches (7.5 cm) wide.

First Hump

This piece starts at the top of the hump, using Pillar Red yarn.

R1: 6 sc in MR (6)

R2: 1 inc in each st (12)

R3: [1 sc, 1 inc] x6 (18)

R4–5: 1 sc in each st (18)

Slst in next st and fasten off. There is no need to weave in the ends; the yarn will end up inside the piece.

Second Hump

This piece starts at the top of the hump, using Pillar Red yarn.

R1: 6 sc in MR (6)

R2: 1 inc in each st (12)

R3: [1 sc, 1 inc] x6 (18)

R4–5: 1 sc in each st (18)

Leaving your hook in the last stitch, continue to the next piece.

(continued)

Heart Body

Hold the two humps together as shown. With the last loop of the second hump still on your hook, slst 1 through both pieces to join. For the next round, crochet clockwise around both pieces, excluding the slst used to join.

R1: 17 sc around the second hump, 17 sc around the first hump (34)

R2: 3 sc, 1 dec, 7 sc, 1 dec, 6 sc, 1 dec, 7 sc, 1 dec, 3 sc (30)

R3: [8 sc, 1 dec] x3 (27)

R4: [7 sc, 1 dec] x3 (24)

R5: [6 sc, 1 dec] x3 (21)

R6: [5 sc, 1 dec] x3 (18)

R7: [4 sc, 1 dec] x3 (15)

R8: [3 sc, 1 dec] x3 (12)

Place the eyes between R4 and R5, about 4 stitches apart. Using black yarn, embroider the mouth onto the front of the face, just below the eyes, using the tapestry needle. Stuff the piece with polyester fiberfill.

R9: [2 sc, 1 dec] x3 (9)

R10: [1 sc, 1 dec] x3 (6)

Close off, and then hide the yarn end with a tapestry needle.

Heart body, joining

Valentina the Heart, finished

Peep the Bunny

The sugary, sticky, sweet marshmallow Peeps® are an iconic treat to fill your Easter basket. I know they're not everyone's favorite candy, but they're still pretty adorable. We also have a bunny at home named Reese, after another classic chocolate Easter treat. Peep the Bunny can be made in a variety of colors and is just as sweet as his candy counterparts. Peep is worked in continuous rounds, starting with the ears. Then, the ears are joined together to create a seamless piece with no sewing necessary. This technique may be a little tricky on your first try, so set aside some extra time, if needed. Peep's finished size is about 5 inches (12.5 cm) tall and 2½ inches (6.5 cm) wide.

First Ear

This piece starts at the top of the ear, using Pale Lilac yarn.

R1: 6 sc in MR (6)

R2: 1 inc in each st (12)

R3–8: 1 sc in each (12)

Slst in next st and fasten off. There is no need to weave in the ends; the yarn will end up inside the piece.

Second Ear

This piece starts at the top of the ear, using Pale Lilac yarn.

R1: 6 sc in MR (6)

R2: 1 inc in each st (12)

R3–8: 1 sc in each (12)

Leaving your hook in the last stitch, continue to the next piece.

(continued)

Body

Hold the two ears together as shown. With the last loop of the second ear still on your hook, slst 1 through both pieces to join. For the next round, crochet clockwise around both pieces, excluding the slst used to join.

R1: 11 sc around the second ear, 11 sc around the first ear (22)

R2: 5 sc, 1 inc, 10 sc, 1 inc, 5 sc (24)

R3: [7 sc, 1 inc] x3 (27)

R4: 1 sc in each st (27)

R5: [7 sc, 1 dec] x3 (24)

R6: [2 sc, 1 dec] x6 (18)

R7: [1 sc, 1 dec] x6 (12)

Place the eyes between R4 and R5, about 4 stitches apart. Using black yarn, embroider the mouth onto the front of the face, just below the eyes, using a tapestry needle. Stuff the piece with polyester fiberfill.

R8: Working in FLO, [1 sc, 1 inc] x6 (18)

R9: [2 sc, 1 inc] x6 (24)

R10: [3 sc, 1 inc] x6 (30)

R11–12: 1 sc in each st (30)

R13: [3 sc, 1 dec] x6 (24)

R14: [2 sc, 1 dec] x6 (18)

R15: [1 sc, 1 dec] x6 (12)

Stuff the piece with polyester fiberfill.

R16: 6 dec (6)

Close off, and then hide the yarn end with a tapestry needle.

Body, joining

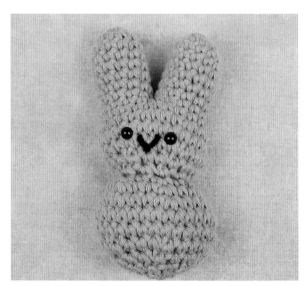

Peep the Bunny, finished

Patch the Pumpkin

As with many families, carving pumpkins for Halloween has always been a tradition for us. Every year my dad would go all out with intricate designs and his own special carving kit, while the kids just cut out simple triangles to make goofy faces. But year after year, we got better and better. Now we all live apart, but the tradition carries on. We still can't keep up with Dad, but it's fun to try. Patch the Pumpkin may be too cute to carve, but you're guaranteed to love this quick and easy pattern that uses a few simple embroidery tricks to create its ridges. The leaf and vine are added last. Set him atop your mantle for the perfect fall decor! Patch's finished size is approximately 2 inches (5 cm) tall and 3 inches (7.5 cm) wide.

Pumpkin

This piece starts at the top of the pumpkin, using Blood Orange yarn.

R1: 6 sc in MR (6)

R2: 1 inc in each st (12)

R3: [1 sc, 1 inc] x6 (18)

R4: [2 sc, 1 inc] x6 (24)

R5: [3 sc, 1 inc] x6 (30)

R6: [4 sc, 1 inc] x6 (36)

R7-10: 1 sc in each st (36)

Place the eyes between R8 and R9, about 4 stitches apart. Using black yarn, embroider the mouth onto the front of the face, just below the eyes, using the tapestry needle.

(continued)

R11: [4 sc, 1 dec] x6 (30)

R12: [3 sc, 1 dec] x6 (24)

R13: [2 sc, 1 dec] x6 (18)

R14: [1 sc, 1 dec] x6 (12)

Stuff the piece lightly with polyester fiberfill to leave room for the ridges to be formed.

R15: 6 dec (6)

Close off and leave a long tail to embroider 6 lines from top to bottom, spaced evenly around the pumpkin. Pull tightly to create the ridges, then tie off and weave in ends.

Leaf and Vine

This piece starts at the base of the leaf, using Grass Green yarn.

Ch 6,

R1: Starting at the second chain from the hook, 1 slst, 1 sc, 1 hdc, 1 sc, 1 slst in the back loops, ch 1, rotate the chain, 1 slst, 1 sc, 1 hdc, 1 sc, 1 slst in the front loops, then ch 13, starting at the second chain from the hook, 12 sc in the back loops.

Ch 1 and fasten off, leaving a short tail. Use the yarn tail to attach the leaf and vine to the top of the pumpkin.

Pumpkin, finished

Leaf and vine, finished

Patch the Pumpkin, finished

Salem the Cauldron

My all-time favorite Halloween movie is *Hocus Pocus*, and seeing this pattern always makes me think of the iconic trio of quirky witches standing over their bubbling cauldron. Salem the Cauldron is worked in continuous rounds and uses a couple of special techniques to make it go quickly, which may take some getting used to. The handles are made first and then worked into the cauldron. Then, the brim of the cauldron is made by folding over the lip and working through two rows together. Salem's finished size is approximately 3 inches (7.5 cm) tall and 3 inches (7.5 cm) wide.

Handles (x2)

This piece starts at the edge of the handle, using Pale Lilac yarn to create an oval. Repeat until you have two handles.

Ch 4,

R1: Starting at the second chain from the hook, sc 3 in the back loops, rotate the chain, then sc 3 in the front loops (6)

R2: Ch 1, flatten the piece, then working through front and backstitches together, 3 sc (3)

Ch 1 and fasten off. There is no need to weave in the ends; the yarn will end up inside the piece.

(continued)

Handles, finished

Cauldron

This piece starts at the top of the cauldron, using Pistachio yarn.

R1: 6 sc in MR (6)

R2: 1 inc in each st (12)

R3: [1 sc, 1 inc] x6 (18)

R4: [2 sc, 1 inc] x6 (24)

R5: [3 sc, 1 inc] x6 (30)

Switch to Pale Lilac yarn.

R6: Working in FLO, 1 sc in each st (30)

R7: [4 sc, 1 inc] x6 (36)

R8: 1 sc in each st (36)

R9: [4 sc, 1 dec] x6 (30)

Fold over the lip as shown.

R10: Working through R9 and the BLO from R5, 1 sc in each st (30)

R11: [4 sc, 1 inc] x6 (36)

R12: [5 sc, 1 inc] x6 (42)

R13: 9 sc, working through one of the handles and the cauldron together, 3 sc, then 18 sc, working through one of the handles and the cauldron together, 3 sc, then 9 sc (42)

R14–17: 1 sc in each st (42)

R18: [5 sc, 1 dec] x6 (36)

R19: [4 sc, 1 dec] x6 (30)

R20: [3 sc, 1 dec] x6 (24)

R21: [2 sc, 1 dec] x6 (18)

R22: [1 sc, 1 dec] x6 (12)

Place the eyes between R15 and R16, about 4 stitches apart. Using black yarn, embroider the mouth onto the front of the face, just below the eyes, using the tapestry needle. Stuff the piece with polyester fiberfill.

R23: 6 dec (6)

Close off, and then hide the yarn end with a tapestry needle.

Cauldron, round 10 (with the lip folded over)   *Cauldron, round 13*

Salem the Cauldron, finished

Candace the Candy Corn

I know people either love or hate candy corn, but I think it's the nostalgia factor that wins me over. It's such a classic sweet Halloween treat that I had to make a crochet version. Plus, I was able to name this pattern after my mom! She honestly has nothing to do with candy corn, but I'll take whatever chance I can to acknowledge this strong, sassy and selfless woman. Candace the Candy Corn is a quick and fun pattern that will work up in no time. Candace's finished size is approximately 3 inches (7.5 cm) tall and 2½ inches (6.5 cm) wide.

Candy Corn

This piece starts at the bottom of the candy corn, using Buttercup Yellow yarn to create an oval.

Ch 7,

R1: Starting at the second chain from the hook, 5 sc and 1 inc in the back loops, rotate the chain, then 5 sc and 1 inc in the front loops (14)

R2: [sc 3 in next, 5 sc, sc 3 in next] x2 (22)

R3: [1 sc, sc 3 in next, 7 sc, sc 3 in next, 1 sc] x2 (30)

R4–5: 1 sc in each st (30)

R6: [1 sc, 1 dec, 9 sc, 1 dec, 1 sc] x2 (26)

Switch to Blood Orange yarn.

R7: 1 sc in each st (26)

R8: [1 sc, 1 dec, 7 sc, 1 dec, 1 sc] x2 (22)

R9: 1 sc in each st (22)

R10: [1 sc, 1 dec, 5 sc, 1 dec, 1 sc] x2 (18)

(continued)

Switch to Paper White yarn.

R11: 1 sc in each st (18)

R12: [1 sc, 1 dec, 3 sc, 1 dec, 1 sc] x2 (14)

R13: 1 sc in each st (14)

Place the eyes between R5 and R6, about 4 stitches apart. Using black yarn, embroider the mouth onto the front of the face, just below the eyes, using the tapestry needle. Stuff the piece with polyester fiberfill.

R14: [1 sc, 1 dec, 1 sc, 1 dec, 1 sc] x2 (10)

R15: 5 dec (5)

Close off, and then hide the yarn end with a tapestry needle.

Candace the Candy Corn, finished

Skill Level: 3

Materials

1 oz Paintbox Yarns Cotton Aran in Soft Fudge (or similar worsted weight/ aran yarn)

0.5 oz Paintbox Yarns Cotton Aran in Paper White (or similar worsted weight/ aran yarn)

Size E-4 (3.5-mm) crochet hook

Stitch marker for marking the first st

2 (¼" [6-mm]) black plastic safety eyes

Scrap piece of black yarn for embroidery

Polyester fiberfill

Tapestry needle

Terminology

R1: row 1 or round 1

st(s): stitch(es)

ch: chain

slst: slip stitch

sc: single crochet

inc: single crochet increase

dec: invisible decrease

MR: magic ring

FLO: front loops only

John Dough the Gingerbread Man

As you all know by now, I love getting crafty! So, decorating gingerbread men and Christmas cookies is always a blast for me, especially with friends and family. But we tend to get a little competitive, so watch out! John Dough the Gingerbread Man is one of the more challenging designs in this book, so set aside some extra time, if needed. The legs are joined together seamlessly, then the arms are worked into the body to eliminate the need for sewing. John's finished size is approximately 5½ inches (14 cm) tall and 3 inches (7.5 cm) wide.

Arms (x2)

This piece starts at the tip of each arm, using Soft Fudge yarn. Repeat until you have 2 arms.

R1: 6 sc in MR (6)

R2: [1 sc, 1 inc] x3 (9)

Switch to Paper White yarn.

R3: 1 sc in each st (9)

Switch to Soft Fudge yarn.

R4–5: 1 sc in each st (9)

R6: [1 sc, 1 dec] x3 (6)

R7: Ch 1, flatten the piece, then working through the front and backstitches together, sc 3 (3)

Ch 1 and fasten off. There is no need to weave in the ends; the yarn will end up inside the piece.

(continued)

First Leg

This piece starts at the bottom of the leg, using Soft Fudge yarn.

R1: 6 sc in MR (6)

R2: 1 inc in each st (12)

Switch to Paper White yarn.

R3: 1 sc in each st (12)

Switch to Soft Fudge yarn.

R4-7: 1 sc in each st (12)

Slst in next st and fasten off. There is no need to weave in the ends; the yarn will end up inside the piece.

Second Leg

This piece starts at the bottom of the leg, using Soft Fudge yarn.

R1: 6 sc in MR (6)

R2: 1 inc in each st (12)

Switch to Paper White yarn.

R3: 1 sc in each st (12)

Switch to Soft Fudge yarn.

R4-7: 1 sc in each st (12)

Leaving your hook in the last stitch, continue to the next piece.

Body

Hold the two legs together as shown. With the last loop of the second leg still on your hook, slst 1 through both pieces to join. For the next round, crochet clockwise around both pieces, excluding the slst used to join.

R1: 11 sc around the second leg, 11 sc around the first leg (22)

R2: 5 sc, 1 inc, 10 sc, 1 inc, 5 sc (24)

R3-4: 1 sc in each st (24)

Arm, finished

Body, joining

R5: [6 sc, 1 dec] x3 (21)

R6: [5 sc, 1 dec] x3 (18)

R7: [4 sc, 1 dec] x3 (15)

R8: [3 sc, 1 dec] x3 (12)

R9: 3 sc, working through an arm and the body together, sc 3, then 3 sc, working through an arm and the body together, sc 3 (12)

R10: 1 sc in each st (12)

Stuff the piece with polyester fiberfill.

R11: Working in FLO, [1 sc, 1 inc] x6 (18)

R12: [2 sc, 1 inc] x6 (24)

R13: [3 sc, 1 inc] x6 (30)

R14: [4 sc, 1 inc] x6 (36)

R15–18: 1 sc in each st (36)

R19: [4 sc, 1 dec] x6 (30)

R20: [3 sc, 1 dec] x6 (24)

R21: [2 sc, 1 dec] x6 (18)

R22: [1 sc, 1 dec] x6 (12)

Place the eyes between R15 and R16, about 4 stitches apart. Using black yarn, embroider the mouth onto the front of the face, just below the eyes, using the tapestry needle. Stuff the piece with polyester fiberfill.

R23: 6 dec (6)

Close off, and then hide the yarn end with a tapestry needle.

Body, round 9

John Dough the Gingerbread Man, finished

Jack the Snowman

When my siblings and I were kids, we'd go up to the mountains for a weekend in the snow. We'd line up behind our uncle and ski down the mountain like a row of ducks. Then, we'd head back to the cabin to build and accessorize our snowman while the adults prepared dinner. Just like our real snowman, Jack the Snowman is dressed to impress with his pom-pom hat and scarf! His keen fashion style might make this pattern seem a little intimidating, but he was thoughtfully designed to work up quickly. Jack's finished size is approximately 5 inches (12.5 cm) tall and 2½ inches (6.5 cm) wide.

Snowman

This piece starts at the top of the hat, using Pillar Red yarn.

R1: 6 sc in MR (6)

R2: 1 inc in each st (12)

R3: [1 sc, 1 inc] x6 (18)

R4: [2 sc, 1 inc] x6 (24)

R5-6: 1 sc in each st (24)

Switch to Paper White yarn.

R7: Working in BLO, 1 sc in each st (24)

R8-9: 1 sc in each st (24)

R10: [2 sc, 1 dec] x6 (18)

R11: [1 sc, 1 dec] x6 (12)

Place the eyes between R8 and R9, about 4 stitches apart. Using black yarn, embroider the mouth onto the front of the face, just below the eyes, using the tapestry needle. Stuff the piece with polyester fiberfill.

(continued)

R 12: Working in FLO, [1 sc, 1 inc] x6 (18)

R 13: [2 sc, 1 inc] x6 (24)

R 14: [3 sc, 1 inc] x6 (30)

R 15–18: 1 sc in each st (30)

R 19: [3 sc, 1 dec] x6 (24)

R 20: [2 sc, 1 dec] x6 (18)

R 21: [1 sc, 1 dec] x6 (12)

Stuff the piece with polyester fiberfill.

R 22: 6 dec (6)

Close off, and then hide the yarn end with a tapestry needle.

Brim

Using Pillar Red yarn, join the yarn to the first front loop of R6 left behind from R7 of the snowman, ch 1, then start your first stitch in the same stitch as the join.

R 1: Working in FLO of R6, 1 hdc in each st (24)

Slst in next st. Fasten off and weave in the ends with a tapestry needle.

Scarf

This piece starts at one end of the scarf, using Pillar Red yarn.

Ch 46,

R 1: Starting at the second chain from the hook, 45 sc (45)

Ch 1 and fasten off. Weave in the ends with a tapestry needle. Tie the scarf around the snowman's neck.

Pom-pom

Using Paper White yarn, wrap the yarn around the tines of a fork 20 to 30 times. Tie a knot tightly around the middle, leaving the tails long.

Carefully slide the yarn off the fork. Cut the loops and shape the pom-pom, as needed.

Use the yarn tails to attach the pom-pom to the top of the hat.

Brim, joining

Scarf, finished

Pom-pom, wrapping the yarn

Pom-pom, cutting the loops

Pom-pom, finished

Jack the Snowman, finished

Skill Level: 2

Materials

0.5 oz Paintbox Yarns Cotton Aran in Paper White (or similar worsted weight/aran yarn)

0.5 oz Paintbox Yarns Cotton Aran in Pillar Red (or similar worsted weight/aran yarn)

Size E-4 (3.5-mm) crochet hook

Stitch marker for marking the first st

2 (¼" [6-mm]) black plastic safety eyes

Scrap piece of black yarn for embroidery

Polyester fiberfill

Tapestry needle

Terminology

R1: row 1 or round 1

st(s): stitch(es)

sc: single crochet

inc: single crochet increase

dec: invisible decrease

MR: magic ring

Patty the Peppermint Candy

After pumpkin spice season, it's time for peppermint season! Peppermint candy, candy canes and peppermint mochas are a must. My personal favorite is making chocolate peppermint bark with crushed-up pieces of peppermint candy. You won't be able to eat Patty the Peppermint Candy, but she is still as sweet as can be with her little smile. Patty is worked in continuous rounds and comes together quickly. But the design requires a lot of color changes, which may take some getting used to. Set aside some extra time for your first try, if needed. Patty's finished size is approximately 2½ inches (6.5 cm) in diameter and 1½ inches (4 cm) thick.

Peppermint Candy

This piece starts at the center of the candy, using Paper White yarn.

R1: 6 sc in MR (6)

R2: 1 inc in each st (12)

R3: [1 sc, 1 inc] x6 (18)

R4: [2 sc, 1 inc] x6 (24)

The next few rounds will require color changes between Pillar Red and Paper White as indicated below. Refer to page 143 for more information on color changes. There is no need to cut the old color and tie the ends together inside the piece; just drop the yarn inside the piece when it is not being used and pick up the yarn again for the next color change.

R5: [Using red yarn, 2 sc, then using white yarn, 1 sc, 1 inc] x6 (30)

R6: [Using red yarn, 1 sc, 1 inc, then using white yarn, 3 sc] x6 (36)

R7–8: [Using red yarn, 3 sc, then using white yarn, 3 sc] x6 (36)

Place the eyes between R2 and R3, about 4 stitches apart. Using black yarn, embroider the mouth onto the front of the face, just below the eyes, using the tapestry needle.

(continued)

R9: [Using red yarn, 1 sc, 1 dec, then using white yarn, 3 sc] x6 (30)

R10: [Using red yarn, 2 sc, then using white yarn, 1 sc, 1 dec] x6 (24)

Continue with Paper White yarn.

R11: [2 sc, 1 dec] x6 (18)

R12: [1 sc, 1 dec] x6 (12)

Stuff the piece with polyester fiberfill.

R13: 6 dec (6)

Close off, and then hide the yarn end with a tapestry needle.

Patty the Peppermint Candy, finished

Melody the Bell

When we were kids, my parents hosted big, extravagant Christmas parties with all their friends. My dad would dress up as Hawaiian Santa Claus, complete with an aloha shirt and flip flops, and hand out goodie bags with all the bells and whistles . . . literally! My mom would purposely buy the loudest, messiest and most obnoxious toys she could find to mess with the other parents. She really took the idea of "jingle all the way" to heart! Melody the Bell is blissfully quiet in comparison. She is worked in continuous rounds, and the bottom of the bell is made by folding over the lip and working through two rows together. Melody's finished size is approximately 3 inches (7.5 cm) tall and 2½ inches (6.5 cm) wide.

Bell

This piece starts at the top of the bell using Daffodil Yellow yarn.

R1: 6 sc in MR (6)

R2: 1 inc in each st (12)

R3: [1 sc, 1 inc] x6 (18)

R4: [2 sc, 1 inc] x6 (24)

R5–9: 1 sc in each st (24)

R10: [7 sc, 1 inc] x3 (27)

R11: [1 inc, 8 sc] x3 (30)

R12: Working in FLO, [9 sc, 1 inc] x3 (33)

R13: Working in BLO, [9 sc, 1 sc2tog] x3 (30)

(continued)

Fold over the lip as shown.

R14: Working through R13 and the BLO from R11, [3 sc, 1 sc2tog] x6 (24)

R15: [2 sc, 1 dec] x6 (18)

R16: [1 sc, 1 dec] x6 (12)

Place the eyes between R8 and R9, about 4 stitches apart. Using black yarn, embroider the mouth onto the front of the face, just below the eyes, using the tapestry needle. Stuff the piece with polyester fiberfill.

R17: 6 dec (6)

R18: 1 inc in each st (12)

R19: 6 dec (6)

Close off, and then hide the yarn end with a tapestry needle. To hang the bell, use a scrap piece of Daffodil Yellow yarn to create a loop at the top of the piece. Hide the yarn ends with a tapestry needle.

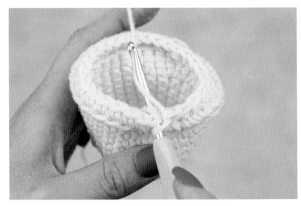

Bell, round 14 (with the lip folded over)

Melody the Bell, finished

Materials

0.5 oz Paintbox Yarns Cotton Aran in Pure Black (or similar worsted weight/aran yarn)

0.5 oz Paintbox Yarns Cotton Aran in Pillar Red (or similar worsted weight/aran yarn)

0.5 oz Paintbox Yarns Cotton Aran in Buttercup Yellow (or similar worsted weight/aran yarn)

0.5 oz Paintbox Yarns Cotton Aran in Kingfisher Blue (or similar worsted weight/aran yarn)

Size E-4 (3.5-mm) crochet hook

Stitch marker for marking the first st

2 (¼" [6-mm]) black plastic safety eyes

Scrap piece of black yarn for embroidery

Polyester fiberfill

Tapestry needle

Tink the Christmas Lights

During the holiday season, I love driving out to Candy Cane Lane to look at all the extravagant light displays. My favorite house reserves a radio station where you can listen to their Christmas playlist from your car as the lights dance along to the music. I wanted to bring home a bit of that magic, so I decided to design Tink the Christmas Lights! Tink is an adorably fun pattern joined together by a series of chain stitches and calls for three lights, but you can string together as many as you like. Because there are a few components needed, you may want to set aside some extra time for your first try. Tink's finished size is approximately 2½ inches (6.5 cm) tall and 1 inch (2.5 cm) wide for each light. A chain of 3 lights is approximately 5 inches (12.5 cm) wide.

Terminology

R1: row 1 or round 1

st(s): stitch(es)

ch: chain

slst: slip stitch

sc: single crochet

inc: single crochet increase

dec: invisible decrease

MR: magic ring

FLO: front loops only

BLO: back loops only

Lightbulb (x3)

This piece starts at the top of the lightbulb, using Pure Black yarn. Repeat until you have 3 lightbulbs in your choice of colors.

R1: 6 sc in MR (6)

R2: 1 inc in each st (12)

R3: Working in BLO, 1 sc in each st (12)

R4: 1 sc in each st (12)

Switch to Pillar Red yarn, Buttercup Yellow yarn, Kingfisher Blue yarn or the color of your choice.

(continued)

R5: Working in FLO, [1 sc, 1 inc] x6 (18)

R6: [5 sc, 1 inc] x3 (21)

R7: [6 sc, 1 inc] x3 (24)

R8: 1 sc in each st (24)

R9: [6 sc, 1 dec] x3 (21)

R10: [5 sc, 1 dec] x3 (18)

R11: [4 sc, 1 dec] x3 (15)

R12: [3 sc, 1 dec] x3 (12)

Wire, joining yarn

Place the eyes between R8 and R9, about 4 stitches apart. Using black yarn, embroider the mouth onto the front of the face, just below the eyes, using the tapestry needle. Stuff the piece with polyester fiberfill.

R13: [2 sc, 1 dec] x3 (9)

R14: [1 sc, 1 dec] x3 (6)

Close off, and then hide the yarn end with a tapestry needle.

Wire

Using Pure Black yarn, join yarn to the top of one of the bulbs. Then, ch 10, slst through the top of the next bulb, ch 10, slst through the top of the last bulb.

Ch 1 and fasten off. Weave in the ends with a tapestry needle.

Tink the Christmas Lights, finished

Skill Level: 2

Materials

1 oz Paintbox Yarns Cotton Aran in Grass Green (or similar worsted weight/aran yarn)

Size E-4 (3.5-mm) crochet hook

Stitch marker for marking the first st

2 (¼" [6-mm]) black plastic safety eyes

Scrap piece of black yarn for embroidery

Scrap piece of red yarn for details

Polyester fiberfill

Tapestry needle

Terminology

R1: row 1 or round 1

st(s): stitch(es)

ch: chain

slst: slip stitch

sc: single crochet

hdc: half double crochet

inc: single crochet increase

dec: invisible decrease

Douglas the Wreath

I love the smell of fresh pine, and every year my husband and I go Christmas tree shopping for the biggest and fluffiest tree we can find. Then sometimes, I'll clip the extra branches at the bottom of the tree to make a wreath so I can spread that fresh pine smell all over the house. Douglas the Wreath won't smell as good as the real thing, but he's adorable and works up quickly once you get the hang of it. Douglas starts with a chain and is worked in continuous rounds, then joined together to create a donut shape. Then, we add a ruffle and a red bow to complete the look. Douglas's finished size is approximately 4½ inches (11.5 cm) in diameter and 1½ inches (4 cm) thick.

Wreath

This piece starts at the outside edge of the wreath, using Grass Green yarn.

Ch 48, then start R1 in the first chain, creating a loop.

R1: 1 sc in each st (48)

(continued)

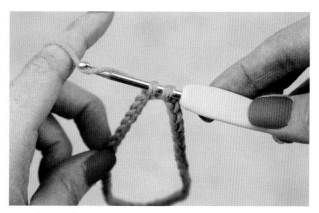

Wreath, round 1

R2: [6 sc, 1 dec] x6 (42)

R3: [1 dec, 5 sc] x6 (36)

R4: [4 sc, 1 dec] x6 (30)

R5: [1 dec, 3 sc] x6 (24)

R6–8: 1 sc in each st (24)

R9: [1 inc, 3 sc] x6 (30)

R10: [4 sc, 1 inc] x6 (36)

R11: [1 inc, 5 sc] x6 (42)

R12: [6 sc, 1 inc] x6 (48)

R13: 1 sc in each st (48)

Wreath, round 14

Place the eyes between R10 and R11, about 4 stitches apart. Using black yarn, embroider the mouth onto the front of the face, just below the eyes, using the tapestry needle.

R14: Working through R13 and the foundation chain together and stuffing periodically, 1 sc in each st (48)

R15: [1 slst, skip 1 st, 5 hdc in next, skip 1 st] x12

Slst in next st. Fasten off and weave in the ends with a tapestry needle.

Using red yarn, tie a bow to the bottom of the wreath.

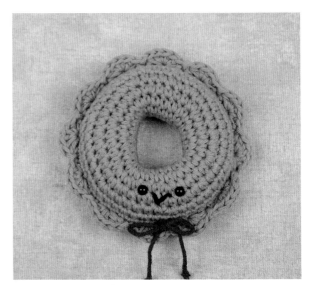

Douglas the Wreath, finished

The Basics

This chapter goes over all the basics to get you started, including selecting the best tools and materials to use for this book, such as type of yarn and hook size. I'll also cover all the stitches you'll use, from simple things such as the single crochet, to unique no-sew techniques, including crocheting through multiple pieces or the seamless join. If you are new to amigurumi, I recommend practicing some of the stitches and techniques until you are comfortable with the motions before diving into the projects. Even experienced crocheters may not be familiar with the tips and tricks I use to cut down on time and minimize sewing, so I still recommend taking a peek before you get started. It may feel awkward at first, but I promise you'll get the hang of it! Your pieces may not look exactly the same, but that's what makes each one special and unique.

Tools and Materials

These tools and materials are all you need to make the projects in this book—and good news! They're pretty inexpensive and readily available in most craft stores or online, which makes it easy to get started with amigurumi! There are hundreds of variations for each item, but they all function in more or less the same way. My recommendations are mentioned, but feel free to try out different brands, styles and sizes to find what you like best.

Yarn

I typically use worsted weight/Aran yarn in cotton or acrylic for my designs. Paintbox Yarns in Cotton Aran is one of my favorites and is used throughout this book. The yarns are beautifully soft with lots of color options. Red Heart Super Saver is another great option and is available at most craft stores. When working through the patterns in this book, you can use any yarn material or thickness you like; just keep it consistent throughout each piece. Try Hobbii Baby Snuggle Solid Yarn for fluffy, cuddle-sized pieces, or play around and see what you like best!

Hooks

I use an E-4 (3.5-mm) crochet hook with my worsted weight yarn. I find that tight stitches create a cleaner look, help the piece hold shape and prevent any stuffing from poking through the stitches. But depending on how much tension you hold in your yarn, you may need a bigger or smaller hook size. When I taught my husband to crochet, he held his yarn tension so tight that I had to compensate by giving him a larger hook. So, it may take some trial and error to figure out what works best for you.

Safety Eyes

Safety eyes are available in different shapes and sizes to create unique looks. Just snap on the back washer to hold them in place. All the patterns in this book use ¼-inch (6-mm) diameter black plastic safety eyes, which can be found online.

Stuffing

Polyester fiberfill is available at most craft stores. In the pattern, I identify the crucial points to stuff the piece, but I recommend stuffing periodically as you go to ensure an even distribution. Feel free to stuff to your likeness, but avoid overstuffing, as it will stretch out the stitches.

Tapestry Needle

This large, blunt-ended needle makes embroidery and finishing off a breeze. I like the ones with a bent tip for better maneuverability.

Stitch Markers

Stitch markers come in many different shapes and sizes, but their main purpose is to mark the end of the row or round, so you don't lose your spot or to hold your stitch when you set down your project. If you don't have stitch markers, just use a scrap piece of yarn, a paper clip or a safety pin.

Stitches and Techniques

Once you have all the materials, it's time to learn how to bring them all together, including a few special tips and techniques to cut down on time and minimize sewing.

Handling the Hook and Yarn

First up, the two most common ways to hold a crochet hook are the "pencil grip" and the "knife grip." I typically like to use the "knife grip" in my right hand, as you'll see in photos throughout this book. But, as long as the stitches work up correctly, there is no right or wrong way. Play around with what feels comfortable. With your other hand, hold the working piece between your thumb and middle finger. Drape the yarn over your index finger and through your hand to control tension. Gauge (how big your stitches are) is not particularly important as long as you are maintaining consistent tension in the yarn.

As you're working, be sure to pay attention to the "right" (front) and "wrong" (back) sides of your amigurumi. When working in rounds, the "right" side is the side facing you where the face of each stitch creates a V shape. The "wrong" side faces away from you where the face of each stitch creates a horizontal bar. It's common for your amigurumi piece to curl in, so you may need to curl it away from you while you work or flip it inside out at the end if you want the "right" side to face outward. Either way is acceptable, and it is generally a matter of personal preference. But my patterns and photos show the designs with the "right" side facing outward, so it may get confusing if you choose a different approach.

If you make a mistake, just remove your hook, pull the yarn end and the piece will unravel. This process is called frogging. Undo the piece until your mistake is gone, and then pick up where the pattern left off. Mistakes happen and luckily, they're easy to fix in amigurumi!

Pencil grip

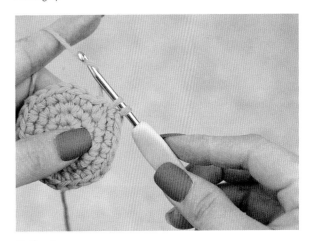
Knife grip

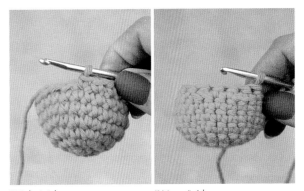
"Right" side   *"Wrong" side*

Reading Patterns

One of the trickiest parts of crochet is making sense of all the terminology and abbreviations—it's almost like learning a new language! But every pattern typically has the same few components. At the beginning of each project, I list all the stitches and abbreviations you need to know so you can quickly reference this chapter. As we work through the pattern, each line starts with the Round/Row number, the pattern instructions and the number of stitches completed in the round. For example, "R1: [2 sc, 1 inc] x6 (24)" means that for Round 1, we work 1 single crochet in each of the next 2 stitches. Then, we work 1 increase in the following stitch. The sequence between the brackets should be worked a total of six times and by the end of this round, we will have completed 24 stitches. Note that every designer has their own writing technique, so it may take some getting used to.

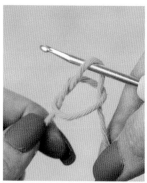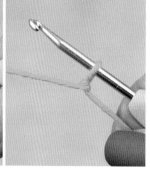

Slipknot

Make a loop with the yarn around your first two fingers. The short end should be in front and the long end in back. Hold the yarn where the two strands meet. Insert the hook into the loop from front to back, pull the yarn through the loop, then tighten the knot.

Yarn Over (YO)

Wrap the yarn over your hook from back to front.

Chain (ch)

With a loop on your hook, YO and pull the yarn through the loop on the hook. When counting your chains, the loop on the hook is omitted.

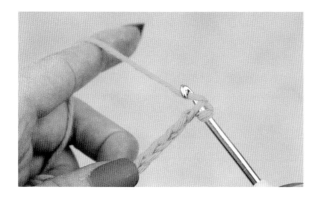

Working in Rows

If you are beginning a new piece, start with a slipknot and then continue to create chains as specified in the pattern. When working into a chain, you typically begin with the second chain from the hook. To start a new row, the pattern will typically call for you to ch 1, turn and continue the work.

Front/Back Loops Only (FLO/BLO)

The top of your stitches will look like a series of Vs. Insert your hook into both strands of the V unless the pattern states otherwise. But, when working in BLO, only insert the hook in the strand farthest from you. When working in FLO, only insert the hook into the strand closest to you.

Slip Stitch (slst)

Insert your hook into the st, YO and pull the yarn through the st and the loop on your hook.

Single Crochet (sc)

This is the most common stitch in amigurumi. Insert your hook into the stitch or chain [sc1]. YO and draw up a loop (pull yarn through st). You should have two loops on your hook. YO again and pull the yarn through both loops on the hook.

Half Double Crochet (hdc)

YO, insert your hook into the st, then YO. Draw up a loop. You should have three loops on your hook. YO again and pull the yarn through all three loops on the hook.

Single Crochet 2 Together (sc2tog)

Insert your hook into the st, YO and draw up a loop. Insert your hook into the next st, YO and draw up a loop. You should have three loops on your hook. YO again and pull the yarn through all three loops on the hook.

Single Crochet 3 Together (sc3tog)

Insert your hook into the st, YO and draw up a loop. Repeat in the next 2 stitches. You should have four loops on your hook. YO again and pull the yarn through all four loops on the hook.

Increase (inc)

Work 2 sc in the same st or ch.

Invisible Decrease (dec)

This can be used interchangeably with sc2tog. However, I prefer an invisible decrease when possible, as it creates a cleaner look. Insert your hook into the FLO of the first st, then insert your hook into the FLO of the next st. YO and draw up a loop. You should have two loops on your hook. YO again and pull the yarn through both loops on the hook.

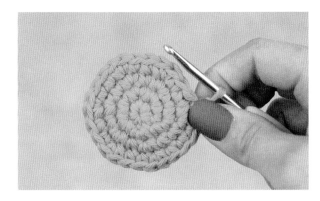

Working in Rounds

Amigurumi is typically crocheted in continuous rounds unless otherwise stated—no turning or joining needed. This creates a nice, clean, seamless look.

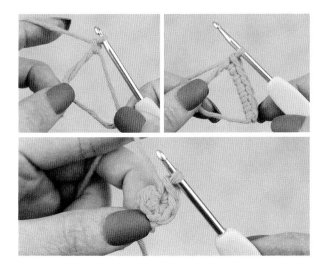

Magic Ring (MR)

The magic ring (or magic circle) is a must for amigurumi. It creates a beautiful clean base to work with when crocheting in continuous rounds. To start, make a loop around your first two fingers. The short end should be in front and the long end in back. Hold the yarn where the two strands meet. Insert the hook into the loop from front to back, YO and draw up a loop, then ch 1. Continue to sc around the loop and yarn tail until you've completed the required amount, then pull the yarn tail to close the hole.

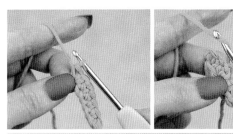

Oval

To create an oval, start with a foundation chain. Create the designated number of chains, then starting at the second chain from the hook, follow the pattern working in BLO, rotate the chain, then follow the pattern working in FLO.

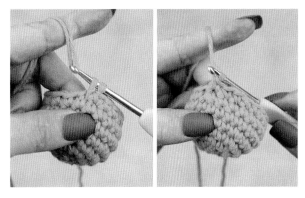

Changing Colors

While still using the original color, stop when you have the last two loops on your hook. With the new color, YO and pull the yarn through both loops. Continue working with the new color. Cut the old color and tie the ends together inside the piece to secure. If there are alternating color changes, there is no need to cut the old color and tie the ends together. Just pick up the yarn again for the next color change.

Flatten and SC

To minimize sewing, many of the projects in this book require you to flatten and sc. Ch 1 and flatten the piece. The yarn end should be on the right and the front and backstitches should line up. Insert your hook into the set of front and backstitches closest to the hook and sc. Continue to sc through the front and backstitches until the piece is closed. Ch 1 and pull the end of the yarn through to fasten off.

Single Crochet through Multiple Pieces

This technique is used to attach flat pieces without the guesswork of pinning and sewing. The add-on piece is worked into the main body by inserting your hook through the add-on piece and the main body together. Then, YO to start your first sc. Continue to sc through both pieces until fully attached.

Join Yarn in Free Loops

To join a new yarn, insert your hook in the st, and then place a slipknot on the hook. Draw the slipknot through the st and ch 1. Start your first stitch in the same stitch as the join.

Seamless Join

To create a seamless join between two pieces, follow the pattern to create your first piece and fasten off. Then follow the pattern to create your second piece. Leaving your hook in the last stitch, hold the two pieces together as shown, with the first piece in front of the second. Then, slst 1 through both pieces to join. For the next round, crochet clockwise around your first piece and then your second piece, excluding the slst used to join.

Embroidery

Embroidery stitches are often used to add details, such as a mouth or eyes. Thread your yarn or embroidery thread onto your tapestry needle. Starting from inside your piece, bring out your needle at one corner of the mouth or eye and insert at the other corner. Bring out your needle in the middle, just below the corners (or higher for the eyes). Pull the needle through the loop and insert the needle at the same point to anchor the stitch. Tie the ends together inside the piece to secure.

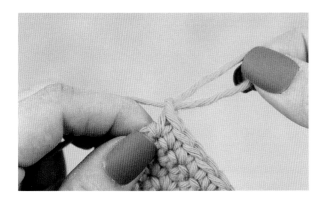

Fasten Off

To fasten off, cut the yarn about 12 inches (30 cm) from your hook and pull the end through the last loop on the hook.

Close Off

To close off when working in rounds, cut the yarn, leaving a long tail, and pull the end through the last loop on the hook. Thread the end of the yarn onto a tapestry needle. Going clockwise through each stitch, insert the needle through the FLO, working from the center of the hole outward. Pull the yarn tight to close the hole. Then, hide the yarn end by inserting your needle through the center of the hole and pulling the end through the body. Cut the excess yarn as close to the fabric as possible, so the cut end will retract back inside the piece.

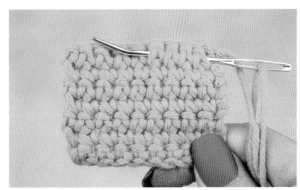

Weave in Ends

Weaving in ends is often not necessary in amigurumi because most of the yarn ends are inside the piece. But for exposed pieces, sew the end through several stitches and cut any excess yarn as close to the piece as possible.

Skill Levels

Each pattern in this book is assigned a skill level between 1 and 3. Beginners are encouraged to start with level 1 projects and work their way up. If you are new to some of the special techniques I use, you may want to set aside a little extra time for level 2 and level 3 patterns. But regardless of skill level, all the projects in this book are fun and unique in their own way! For easy reference, I've organized the projects by skill level so you can develop your plan of attack!

Acknowledgments

I'd like to thank Caitlin and the whole Page Street Publishing team. It has been an absolute pleasure working with you again. I never expected I'd write a book, let alone two! But your guidance, support and trust over the years have made this a dream come true!

Thank you to Paintbox Yarns and LoveCrafts, for providing all the beautifully soft and colorful yarn to create this book.

I'd also like to thank this incredible community of makers. Your continued support over the years means the world to me, and your passion and talent are some of my biggest inspirations.

A huge thank-you to my family and friends. As you can probably see, nearly every pattern in this book was inspired by the memories and experiences we've shared. I truly cherish our time together, and I am so very grateful to have you all in my life.

Last, thank you to my husband, David, for your never-ending love and support. Whenever and however it happens, I can't wait to share this book and all the wonderful memories it holds with our future family. So, when they grow up to be a hurricane of energy, full of big ideas and kind and generous hearts, they'll know it came from their amazing father. In the meantime, thank you for building such a full and happy life for the two of us, filled with endless DIY projects, crazy adventures and our zoo of animals. I love you.

About the Author

Melanie Morita-Hu is the author of *Hooked on Amigurumi* and founder of Knot Too Shabby Crochet, a popular Instagram account and Etsy shop. She began selling amigurumi plushes in 2016, and she has also sold her work at a number of events and festivals.

When Melanie is not crocheting, she's working full time as a civil engineer or helping her husband build out their urban homestead, which has been affectionately dubbed the Hu Zoo. Together they garden, tend to their animals, renovate their home and yard and generally just love working with their hands!

Index